Five Arena Plays

by

MICHAEL MORLEY
MAX ASTRIDGE
ANTHONY DELVES

with

Introduction and Production Notes

by

MICHAEL MORLEY

HEINEMANN EDUCATIONAL
BOOKS LTD · LONDON

Heinemann Educational Books Ltd
LONDON EDINBURGH TORONTO MELBOURNE
SINGAPORE JOHANNESBURG AUCKLAND
NEW DELHI IBADAN NAIROBI
KUALA LUMPUR HONG KONG

ISBN 0 435 23635 0

Introduction and Notes © Michael Morley 1972
First published 1972

Published by
Heinemann Educational Books Ltd
48 Charles Street, London W1X 8AH
Printed in Great Britain by
Cox & Wyman Ltd,
London, Fakenham and Reading

CONTENTS

CONTENTS

INTRODUCTION

ARENA THEATRE is the best experimental training-ground
for young actors. It provides the stimulus of unconventionality,
and, more important, the freedom of movement which all
actors need. Instead of acting to one's front all the time, as is
inevitable on the proscenium stage, the arena encourages full-
circle movement. This is far less inhibiting for the performer;
many actors find they can move more spontaneously 'in the
round' and this frees them to act more convincingly. It also
provides a *rapport* with the audience often limited by stage,
arch and curtains.

The producer of plays in the arena will find that imagina-
tion, creatively used, will more than compensate for the lack
of scenic illusion. He must keep the action or dialogue moving,
or at least turning in the arena, but this is no disadvantage.
There is a distinct three-dimensional quality to all performances in the round. If the proscenium stage is likened to a
picture-frame, then the arena is sculptural. The opposition of
stationary or moving figures is a spatial relationship full of
dramatic tension – at times static, but sometimes revolving
like mobiles!

These five plays were written for and first performed in a
school theatre-in-the-round, at Eastbourne Grammar School,
where for more than ten years annual play-writing competi-
tions have provided original playscripts for performance in the
'Five-in-One' Arena Theatre. The school assembly hall has
the usual proscenium stage, but an arena is created in the
centre of the hall with seating ramped on four sides and lighting slung over the acting area. Written with this arena in

mind, these plays show some of the exciting possibilities of experimental drama in the round. The stage directions indicate that the arena has four corner entrances and an audience on four sides. However, it should not be assumed that the plays can be performed in this way only. They are first and foremost plays to be acted and they will readily adapt for production on other stages, including the orthodox proscenium stage.

Production notes for each play are provided at the end of the book which we hope will be particularly helpful to producers who have little experience of arena presentation. The authors are grateful to past and present members of Eastbourne Grammar School Dramatic Society who have helped to stage these arena plays.

MICHAEL MORLEY

The Children's Crusade

based on the novel The Children's Crusade *by Henry Treece*

BY MICHAEL MORLEY

CHARACTERS

OLD GERARD – *the Hermit*
YOUNG GERARD
JEHAN
MARCEL
ROBERT OF BEAUREGARD
BROTHER MARTIN
THE PIPER
STEPHEN OF CLOYES
WILLIAM LE COCHON
HUGH LE FER

PRINCIPAL CRUSADERS
OTHER CRUSADERS

MUSICIANS
A small percussion group

THE CHILDREN'S CRUSADE

The play is a narrative, and the scene starts in Villacours (central France) and ends in Marseilles. It is mid-summer in the year 1212. The stage is bare except for an old HERMIT, *who gazes round before speaking.*

HERMIT: I seem very old and very strange – a visitor from some other world, perhaps, for my thoughts and feelings were not like yours. Look at me, for I am alien to you – and yet the same flesh and blood. How can you know what life was like in my time, 800 years ago? In my day, the earth stopped at the bounds of Europe, and we knew we might fall off the edge if we ventured too far. Our eyes were lifted to Heaven for we found no lasting comfort in the fleshly world; our eyes, too, could see Hell, the everlasting furnace that consumed and tormented. We believed in devils and witches, in angels and saints, we believed in the blessed sanctity of Holy Places, and we saw the anti-Christ take possession of Jerusalem, Satan's dark servants, the Saracens, overpower our holy land.

In 1212 – as you now call it – I was a proud boy, Gerard, son of Robert of Beauregard Castle. I heard the whispers and the rumours, that spoke of Stephen. It seemed to me as I listened, filled with dreams of holy deeds, that I was being called to a great service; and I ran away . . .

As he speaks, the sound of baying hounds, halloos, shouts and thudding feet can be heard. A boy, GERARD, *runs in, carrying a bundle, and tries to escape, but a* HUNTSMAN *stops him.*

JEHAN: Come along, my young master, stop struggling or it will be all the worse for you.

GERARD: Let go, you filthy serf. Take your hands off me, how dare you touch a nobleman's son.

WALTER: Don't 'ee call us names now, master Gerard, we're acting under your father's orders. We can hold 'ee – and more.

GERARD: You low cowherds, fit only to touch dung . . .

JEHAN: Well, that's you described then, eh? (*Laughs, until* GERARD *bites him.*) Aaagh – you would, would you. Take that, you puppy (*strikes*) and here's something else to . . .

He is about to kick when ROBERT DE BEAUREGARD *enters.*

ROBERT: All right, Jehan, enough. Don't let me see you laying a finger on my son or you'll be whipped soundly.

JEHAN: But, master, you saw . . .

ROBERT: Silence! Stand back . . . Well, Gerard?

GERARD: Yes, father.

ROBERT: Not 'yes, father' you impertinent wretch. Look at me. Why are you here running away? Is not Beauregard enough? Your hawking? Riding? Jousting?

GERARD: No, father.

ROBERT: I promised your mother – ah, you may not leave my lands . . . one day they will be yours . . . why do you run away? Where are you going?

GERARD: To Jerusalem.

ROBERT: Jerusalem! You poor fool!

GERARD: To the Holy Land, father, on a crusade.

ROBERT: Crusade! Idiot boy! I have told you of the last crusade, the hardships, the futility; the Saracens are too strong. We could do nothing except destroy ourselves.

GERARD: Too strong! It is not you, father, that can win God's holy places. The young will . . .

ROBERT: The young! Ah, the young. So that's it. You have been listening to the gossip, the beggars' prattling, the stupid lies about this north-country bumpkin Stephen.

GERARD: It is known by everyone that Stephen goes to Jerusalem, father.

ROBERT: I commanded that no one should speak of this matter. Who has . . .

Enter BROTHER MARTIN, *tutor to Gerard.*

MARTIN: Oh my dear lord, thank God you have found him. Praise be to the blessed holy mother of God. Gerard, how could you betray my trust . . .

ROBERT: So, brother Martin, perhaps you can explain my son's interest in this crack-pot fever that is sweeping the land, this so-called crusade.

GERARD: There are 30,000 children, father, all marching south.

MARTIN: My lord, I did not tell him. Ride into any village, talk to any mother in the district, they will tell you all about the boy Stephen. There is some devil stirring strange wishes in the hearts of people, high and low, tempting them to renounce their holy Christ and follow this arch-demon in the shape of a boy.

ROBERT: A mere son of a shepherd from Cloyes, twelve years old, gathering about him children of all ages, all ranks, some of them nobly born, others from the ditches, all infected by this midsummer madness.

GERARD: You and your grown-up friends, with their armour and chargers, do not save the Holy Land, father. Perhaps *we* . . .

MARTIN: Gerard, my dear young lord, you know not what you say.

ROBERT: *We*, he says! He divides the world into young and old. What can ignorant children do?

The PIPER, *who has been listening, intervenes.*

PIPER: Perhaps I may speak, my lord of Beauregard. Your
brave son is wiser than you give him credit for.

ROBERT: Who is this?

JEHAN: He's been hanging around the village for a day or
two, my lord. Says he's from the north.

PIPER: So he is, my friend. I come from Vendôme, where the
children gathered. I know Stephen of Cloyes and the thousands of children who are following him. They follow
God.

MARTIN: They follow Satan!

PIPER (shrugging): Would innocent pure children follow the
devil? Stephen speaks with the tongues of angels, scores of
priests revere his holiness. He even spoke to King Philip at
the court of St Denis and gave him a letter which came
from Christ in person, and commanded the King to help
Stephen lead the crusade against the Infidel in the Holy
Land.

MARTIN: You lie, jester. The King sent him packing.

PIPER: And Stephen stood on the steps of the Abbey at St
Denis and spoke of his holy voices and his miracles. He
made me see God and the blessed Virgin Mary and all the
saints. When he reaches Marseilles with his children, the
seas will part as they did for Moses, and all will walk bare-
foot to Jerusalem. Stephen has seen it in a vision – and
bishops have blessed him.

ROBERT: So much the worse for them; they are bigger fools
than I took them for. Be off with you, you blabbing weasel,
before I set the hounds on you. Back to your liege-lord!

PIPER: I am a humble servant of Stephen, my lord. Sometimes
I play sweet music, sometimes I seek out the way, always I
serve Stephen and this holy crusade.

MARTIN: Cease your godless mouthing, you in the garments
of a jester. Have done with wanton mockery and go.

PIPER (*smiling*): But Stephen and his children are upon you. Can you not hear them, thousands of children of Paradise.

In the distance they can hear the sound of singing and marching.

WALTER (*who has been out*): Sir, they are coming down the road to the castle. The children, sir! A great army of them, all singing.

ROBERT: The children's crusade, eh? How many of them?

WALTER: Thousands of them, sir. More than I have ever seen in my life before!

MARTIN: By all the saints, one might imagine that the children of Israel themselves were gathering to cross the Red Sea.

The children enter, a long procession of youngsters in all manner of costume. Most carry blankets and sacks slung on their backs. They straggle untidily into the arena singing with real zest their Crusaders' March:

> Children of the beautiful
> > Cru-u-sade
> Saviours of the Holy Land
> > Cru-u-sade
> Marching on toward the south
> > Gre-eat Sea
> Marching on to make men free
> > Me-en free

The PIPER directs them to halt along a line separating them from the adults, and the arena is filled with children, some carrying banners with strange devices and others simple crosses. On a given signal from the PIPER they cease singing.

PIPER: My dear lord of Beauregard, he has come, the boy Stephen has come. Will you lower your drawbridge and let us enter?

ROBERT (*impressed*): I have never refused hospitality to an honest man in my life. If this Stephen means well, let him come forward now.

The PIPER *plays a merry tune, and the cart is pulled in.*
STEPHEN *sits in it – a strange, gaunt young figure. He looks steadily at Robert, who is more amused than anything else by his appearance.*

STEPHEN: Lord of Beauregard, I bless your house and all who follow the teachings of Christ within it.

ROBERT (*ironically*): I thank you, Stephen of Cloyes, and now I shall take the liberty of asking you and your *chosen* friends to enter my feast hall and to join me in a little supper before you go on your way.

MARTIN (*to Gerard*): He should not harbour this young mountebank. Stephen of Cloyes is abroad on the Devil's work, not God's.

STEPHEN: I come to do God's work, Robert; and all who follow me come to do likewise. It will ill become me to accept favours for myself and my twelve disciples while the others go hungry. (*He stands and raises his arms.*) These are all my brothers. We live and love the world together!

One of the CHILDREN *insolently saunters towards Robert and sings:*

> Children of the beautiful Crusade!
> Saviours of the Holy Land Crusade!

and the CHILDREN *burst into song which the combined efforts of* MARTIN, JEHAN *and* WALTER *cannot quell.* STEPHEN *raises his hand for silence.*

STEPHEN (*sitting again*): Let your servants move among my many little ones, who are hungry and crying for food. Give them bread and meat and warming wine. I will accept such an offering, Robert of Villacours, but nothing less.

ROBERT (*infuriated*): It is not the custom for a wanderer to dictate the laws of hospitality. He must be thankful for what he is given.

STEPHEN (*deriding*): The laws of hospitality! I am not bound
by the outworn customs of mankind. A new spirit is
coming, clean and beautiful; away with your old ways; we
have something new! I make my own customs as God
advises me!

MARTIN: Be silent, blasphemous dog! Who are you to speak
of God? Be off with you, back to the sheep-pen you were
born in. And thank the saints you go with a whole hide.
    STEPHEN *silently peels off his shirt to reveal livid and raw
weals on his back.*

STEPHEN: I have already met men who think as you do,
priest. They have left their marks upon me – but not upon
my spirit.

MARTIN: It grieves me that a mere boy should have suffered
so; yet let it be a warning that you play a dangerous game,
Stephen of Cloyes.

STEPHEN: Christ himself played such a game, priest, and you
will remember he too was whipped with scourges.
    MARTIN *is stunned by such comparisons; the* PIPER *intervenes.*

PIPER: Be not afraid, oh little priest! This honest shepherd lad
comes not to steal your place from you. (*To Robert.*) And
be not afraid, Robert of Villacours, that these poor children
shall eat your bread and drink your precious wine. No, they
are too proud to do that, too proud to do anything but
serve Christ and rid his City of the Infidel. A task which
certain knights of valour might be proud to imitate, Robert
of Villacours – a task I shall be proud to help.
    ROBERT *is lost for words; as he finds them,* STEPHEN *rises.*

STEPHEN: Forward, children of God. We march on, and,
though our bellies are empty and our throats are dry, we
will seek new pastures and warmer welcomes. (*He intones.*)
Yea, even though we walk through the valley of death,
fear not, for Thou art with us. (*He speaks.*) We march to

B

Marseilles and the sea that divides to let us through. (*To Gerard, who is held in the grip of Jehan.*) Follow me . . .

GERARD: Master!

ROBERT: Take him to the castle and lock him in the tower! Go back, you rabble, get off my lands!

But the CHILDREN *have started forward, following the lead of the* PIPER *and the cart. As they march, they sing their Crusader song.* MARTIN *and* ROBERT *try to stem the tide but finally give up; the children begin the circular movement, proceeding round and out of the arena to appear again in a never-ending circle.*

At first they trudge boldly but soon they are treading more slowly, perhaps climbing, and their singing changes to whistling – and then to a solo voice with humming. The long line never breaks. Suddenly, as a cymbal sounds, the lights change, the children in the arena 'freeze' and the OLD HERMIT *enters.*

HERMIT: And I did follow Stephen. Within a day of that terrible spurning of the children, I was slipping out of a postern gate and following the trail of the thousands. It was hot and dry tramping, the children reaching the end of a long and tiring day.

He departs as the cymbal sounds again, the lights revert and the CHILDREN *'unfreeze'. The cart appears as the children continue to march and it halts in the centre as one boy shouts – 'It's that boy from the castle'.* GERARD *runs across to meet the cart and collapses in front of Stephen.* STEPHEN *gazes at him unemotionally.*

STEPHEN: I expected you earlier than this. But you come at the right time, for we must rest here. I hope you have eaten today, for we have no food to give you. Yet all things can be achieved by prayer, and maybe God will provide for you in the village yonder.

PIPER: Hold! Everyone. We stay here till dawn, my pretty

lilies. There is water in the stream there, and the villagers
will be kindly. Take the youngest children and beg for food
for them in the name of Jesus and Stephen.

One BOY *steps forward.*

BOY: May we light a fire, Stephen? We can take a brand from
a cottage hearth.

STEPHEN: It is cool after the heat of the day. Do so; while I
pray.

STEPHEN *dismounts and goes out. Here the* CHILDREN *begin
the Camp scene, which is largely improvised. The sequence of
action and dialogue will begin with the fire being made and the
children settling down in and around the arena; it will end with
the violence and* STEPHEN's *entry; but the middle section could
vary in content. A suggested order of events is:*

(a) *as the* CHILDREN *move in and out, bringing wood for the
     fire or unloading their bedding and exploring, a* BOY *starts
     singing – perhaps a folksong with accompaniment (the*
     PIPER?) *and another* CHILD *joins in. The others listen or
     murmur to others. As the song ends, briefly the singers are
     applauded,*

(b) *and one* BOY *starts to talk to his neighbours. Now in groups
     in the arena, the* CHILDREN *talk about the day's marching,
     their memories of home, their hopes on the journey and their
     love for Stephen. Perhaps one boy,* JEAN DE PARCHAT,
     *is less enthusiastic than the others, but the talking reaches a
     climax of hope and faith,*

(c) *and the* PIPER, *sitting quietly at the side, begins to pipe a
     dance tune. One dancer, then another, rises to dance round
     the fire while others begin to clap in time with the music.*

(d) *A squabble flares up during the dance, perhaps between two
     boys arguing over property or drinks. Gradually more of the
     children are drawn into the disagreement until one* BOY
     strikes another. The group erupt into pairs fighting – and

JEAN DE PARCHAT *draws a knife and threatens Gerard.
One boy shouts – 'He's using a knife!' – which stills the
boys, and* STEPHEN *rushes across to receive the blow as*
JEAN DE PARCHAT *lunges forward.*

  STEPHEN *holds up a hand with blood on it. All are silent as
he looks round at them.*

STEPHEN: Like Christ, my master, I go aside to pray, and I
find my followers not simply asleep but stooping to a fight,
a brawl. What do we believe in, brothers? Not the old
ways, killing, maiming, hating. We are the beautiful people!
Only love and forgiveness will conquer all our sins. You
have displeased God. Go down on your knees, O wayward
wicked sinners, and pray for forgiveness. (*The* CHILDREN
kneel, even JEAN DE PARCHAT.)

STEPHEN: God, mighty lord, forgive our sins and bless our
pilgrimage. Do not break thy promise now, O Lord, let
us enter the holy city in triumph, let the waters of the great
sea divide, let us be thy divine holy messengers. (*He turns
to Jean de Parchat.*) Go, Jean de Parchat. Make your way
where you will, for there is no place for you by our side.

JEAN (*rising*): Stephen of Cloyes, I have served you well and
have got little good of it. I left a comfortable home to ride
with you and now I shall return to it. Nor shall I go alone
for there are many who come from my father's lands. We
go gladly. Think of me, Stephen of Cloyes, when next you
need a sword to save you. Your power is perhaps not what
you think. Mayhap the sea will *not* open and let you walk
to the holy land, shepherd-boy. (*Taking up his belongings,
he moves to go out but the Piper stops him.*)

PIPER (*seizing the knife from Jean*): Here! I'll take that!

STEPHEN: No! Give it to Gerard! (*The* PIPER, *realizing that
here he must obey, does so.*) Take it, Gerard. Use it to cut your
bread. There will be no blood shed in my name!

As GERARD *takes the knife,* JEAN DE PARCHAT *goes.*

STEPHEN: Oh God, if I have acted wrongfully, then punish me. But if I have done according to thy will, then strike Jean de Parchat down in his pride, let him lie like a dog in the road.

A BOY *pushes forward to Stephen, carrying a child.*

NICHOLAS: Stephen, Stephen, my brother is sickening; he grows worse. If we do not get help soon, he will die.

PIPER (*sharply*): Lay that child by the roadside if you wish to live yourself. The sickness in his blood is beyond man's aid. He has the plague!

The CHILDREN *draw back in horror.*

NICHOLAS: What must I do, Stephen? (*He is recoiling.*)

STEPHEN: What if one of us should die? We are many and the task is great. Lay him in a ditch. It will be as God wishes.

GERARD: Let me take him to the village, Stephen. (*He steps forward.*) The priest there will help, surely.

STEPHEN: If God wills the plague, it will be so. Take the child if you wish, and tell the priest to care for him in my name. But do not delay, Gerard, for we press on for Marseilles at dawn.

(GERARD *picks up the child and goes out.*)

PIPER: Rest in peace, my little ones. Sleep. Breathe deeply. Can you smell the clean air from the south, taste the sea breezes? One more day and we reach Marseilles, we shall see the blue waters of the great sea – and Stephen will command the waters.

STEPHEN: I will go apart and pray. Sleep, my friends; sleep, children of God. (*He blesses them and goes out.*)

The CHILDREN *settle down to sleep; the light fades until only the glow of the fire is seen. The* HERMIT *enters with a lantern and walks amid the sleepers.*

HERMIT: And so the children slept, tired, hungry, ragged, dirty, but full of faith, full of yearning for the happy end to their journey. The stars above glowed brightly in the still air, the crickets hummed in the throbbing heart of time, and the children slept. While I, young Gerard, stayed awake in the village, holding a crying child in my arms. I stayed in that village till he died and the priest had dared to come and bless his frail corpse. Perhaps the hand of God was there for, when I returned to Stephen, he and the children had marched on, down into the basin of Marseilles.

He goes; a silence is broken by STEPHEN's *voice from a distance, the sound of sea and gulls; and the arena is lighted. The* CHILDREN *who have been sleeping in the arena (and many others at the sides) arise from sleep and, as* STEPHEN *enters and points towards the sea, they move to gaze at this new spectacle.*

STEPHEN (*off arena*): God in his mercy be praised! The sea, the waters of the great sea are there! (*Entering.*) Look, my disciples. Our marching is over. Only come and see this wonder of God, the sun dancing on the waves, the water stretching as far as the eye can see.

(*He stands before the children, arms raised.*)

We are thy chosen servants, O God; many have been called but few have received thy grace to stay until this moment of glory. Praise be!

PIPER (*sinister*): Now for your miracle, Stephen of Cloyes. For now the children await the journey through the sea. Command the waters, O holy one of God.

STEPHEN: My God has spoken to me. He will not betray me. I trust in Him to show his love for us. (*To children.*) Close your eyes, my children, and kneel. Listen to my words, and, as you listen, pray for me. By God's good grace, when I tell you to open your eyes again, they will see the passage to the Holy Land, for the seas will have rolled back.

He stands and opens his arms; the CHILDREN *kneel with clasped hands and closed eyes. The waves can be heard breaking on the shore.*

STEPHEN: In the name of God, in the name of Christian faith, I command you, waters, to part so that we, the true Crusaders of the Holy Cross, may march to do God's work!

(*The* CHILDREN *call out in unison* – Stephen!) (*anxiously*) In the name of God, I command you, waters, to part so that we, the true Crusaders of the Holy Cross, may march to do God's work! (*The* CHILDREN *sit up in prayer and call* – Stephen!) (*desperately*) Hark, rebel waters, to my commandment while there is yet time. Roll back, I order you, or God will punish you and – dry you up! (*The* CHILDREN *stretch out arms and call* – Stephen!)

STEPHEN (*despairingly*): My God, my God, why hast thou forsaken me?

He collapses sobbing; the CHILDREN *cautiously open eyes, lower arms and gaze in consternation. First one boy, then another stands up; a hubbub follows.*

BOY: The sea, the sea, it hasn't changed!

BOY: We have followed a fool, a trickster!

BOY: Stephen has failed, he is a cheat!

PIPER (*advancing*): Cheer up, young master. Every leader must learn the lesson of disappointment. But listen to me . . . (*To children.*) Listen all of you, friends! Have courage and I promise you, you will live to see the Holy Land. Keep quiet, and sit – all of you. (*The* CHILDREN *sit, while* STEPHEN *lies prostrate, still sobbing.*) Now, your faithful friend, the Piper, has not been idle. I have made plans to help you all. (*Smiling.*) I want you to meet two worthy friends of mine.

He plays a tune on his pipe, and, as if signalled, the two MERCHANTS *come forward into the arena.*

WILLIAM: Greetings, my friend, and to all you unhappy children. Alas, alas, what a calamity. My heart bleeds for you.

HUGH: Poor Stephen! Luckily for you, *we* are here!

WILLIAM: Praise be to God that we are both willing and able to help Stephen and his army.

HUGH: We are good Christian men ready to do our bit to help the work of the lord.

STEPHEN: Do you mock me? What can you do?

WILLIAM: Well, dear boy, we have heard of your marvellous journey here and we have met your friend the piper. He has convinced us that our surest way to salvation in paradise is to help you.

HUGH: To offer you our assistance gratis, without payment, for love of God and little children.

STEPHEN (*sullenly, rising*): Tell us how we may reach the Holy Land.

WILLIAM: By ship, Stephen. We have seven ships awaiting in the harbour. You can see their pennants on the topmasts over there. (*He takes* STEPHEN *and points.*) By providence and the grace of God they are all empty and ready to sail. We will carry you to the Land of your soul's desire.

HUGH: We are honoured to serve such as you.

STEPHEN (*excited*): You hear, my people. God has spoken. It is not his wish that we march to subdue the Saracen. We are to take ships there! We are to sail there!

   The CHILDREN *cheer and begin to rise; two sturdy* YOUTHS *hoist Stephen on their shoulders to carry him out in triumph.*

PIPER: This is William Cochon, Stephen, and this is Hugh Lefer, both very good merchants of this port.

STEPHEN (*confidence restored*): William and Hugh, we thank you. You are the true agents of God. I see haloes round your heads. We shall go to your ships at once. My people, follow me!

He is carried out, and the CHILDREN *begin to march out, starting a continual flow of crusaders as they go round to enter the arena again. They sing the second Crusader Song; eventually the line of children diminishes. The* MERCHANTS *beckon the children on; the last crusader is a lame boy who hobbles across.* WILLIAM *raises his eyebrows, but* HUGH *shrugs shoulders, and he too is welcomed. The singing dies away:*
second Crusader Song:

> Children of the great Crusade
> Sailing over the great Sea
> Sunshine smiling down on us
> We are young and we are free
>
> Freedom of the road is ours
> Stephen's words will lead us on
> We believe in all he tells
> Loving all and hating none.
>
> Enemies of God, beware,
> All your hatred now must cease
> Stephen and his children come
> Bringing love and gentle peace
>
> Children of the great Crusade
> etc.

As the PIPER *and the* MERCHANTS *talk and exult,* GERARD *enters and overhears them.*

PIPER: And so the Children's Crusade ends as I knew it would. Poor innocent fools!

WILLIAM: There are not as many as you said, my friend, but still enough to interest the infidel across the sea.

HUGH: Don't worry, William, we shall cover our expenses. If the Moors do not want slave-girls, they will appreciate the Christian children as interpreters and clerks.

WILLIAM: Here is your money, piper. (*He gives him a bag.*) We strike an honest bargain, and you have delivered your side of the deal honestly enough.

PIPER (*counting the contents*): I take it no child will return. They will all be sold into slavery in Africa. I do not wish tale-bearers to follow me northwards.

HUGH: No chance of that. They will disappear from the face of the earth.

WILLIAM: Farewell, my friend.

HUGH: And if you should happen on any more bands of young hopefuls, you know where to find us.

PIPER: Of course. Farewell. But for the moment I shall lie low.

  WILLIAM *and* HUGH *depart. The* PIPER *exultantly holds up his bag of gold and then turns to leave. He sees Gerard.*

PIPER: Hello, it's Gerard of Beauregard. Too late to catch the boat to the Holy Land, eh? What happened to that little lad with the plague?

GERARD: He died. It has taken me two days to find the crusade. Have they all gone down to the ships? (*He is still looking beyond the Piper.*)

PIPER: All. Led by Stephen. It was a goodly sight as they went aboard. (*He pauses, then craftily.*) Did you hear me talking to my two merchant friends, William and Hugh?

GERARD (*suddenly light dawning*): Yes. I heard you say they would all go to slavery. They will not go to the Holy Land.

PIPER: So. Well, no one will believe your tale. Of course they are going to the Holy Land. (*He thrusts Gerard to the ground roughly.*) And you are too late.

GERARD: That bag of gold. You sold Stephen and the children to those merchants!

PIPER: Well, I have gold, it is true. But how I obtained it is another story. I shall not wait to hear it told in Marseilles. Consider yourself fortunate, young Gerard, and go back to your angry father at Beauregard. (*He turns to leave.*)

GERARD: Devil! Your deeds are black as hell itself. You are not fit to touch the smallest of those children. How could you? I hate you!

The PIPER *looks at him and then contemptuously spits; he turns to go.* GERARD, *almost beside himself, pulls the knife from his belt and runs at the Piper with a great cry. The knife strikes home in the Piper's back and, as he falls, he drives it farther into his body. The* PIPER *loses his bag of gold and dies reaching for it.*

PIPER: Aaagh! treachery! My gold!

GERARD is horror-stricken at his action. He kneels by the body, dagger in hand. The arena darkens and then lights the HERMIT *kneeling, praying.*

HERMIT: O Christ who takest away the sins of the world – forgive my sin. Take from my heart the terror and the fear of my evil deed. (*He looks up.*) After I killed the Piper, I ran away – haunted by the murder I had committed. 'Thou shalt not kill' and my guilt is overflowing. I could never return to my old life at Beauregard. I began my travels, gradually I became the person you see now. Stephen and the Children of the crusade – they are in Christ's bosom now, but I must wander the world with my guilt.

You can never know the real meaning of these ancient deeds; but perhaps you can find some pity for me, a sinner. Would you have raised no knife against him?

He is still praying as the lights fade.

Colombo

BY MAX ASTRIDGE

CHARACTERS

OLD MARINER
YOUNG DRUMMER-BOY
JUAN, A SAILOR
1ST SAILOR
2ND SAILOR
CAPTAIN
CHRISTOPHER COLUMBUS
MARTIN PINZON
FRANCISCO PINZON
VINCENTE PINZON
1ST PERSON IN AUDIENCE
2ND PERSON IN AUDIENCE
CREW OF THE 'SANTA MARIA'

COLOMBO

The action of the play takes place just before dawn, 12 October 1492. We are on the high seas sailing westward, but the OLD MARINER *first introduces the scene. As light slowly intensifies, he can be seen lying asleep in the arena. There are the sounds of waves beating on the sides of a ship, sea-gulls crying and timbers creaking as he slowly wakes.*

OLD MARINER: What! – what? – Oh! It's you, is it? You must excuse me for being asleep – but it's understandable, isn't it? What I mean is – well – blow me duffy, that young producer chap asked me to tell you a yarn, sits me down here, with me drop of grog, goes off and presently – out go all the lights. Well, it's natural for an old sailor to nod off a bit, ain't it? And now about this yarn o' mine – well, first as you may see I'm an old salt, born 1492 or thereabouts. Now stop racking your brains as to what happened in that year – I'll tell you, all in good time – all in good time. If I hadn't have run away from that little farm and became a drummer-boy on that ship, beating my drum for the change of watch – why then, history, as the scholars call it, might have been very different. Why? – well now, that's my yarn, d'y' see. Listen then. It all started just before I was agoing to beat for the evening watch. And old Juan was telling me about his green Mermaid.

By now the CREW *has entered, hauling slowly on a rope to the sounds of a shanty, a subdued, rather listless activity. The* CREW *continues to work as* JUAN, *an old sailor, enters talking to the Drummer-boy. The* OLD MARINER *leaves the arena as* JUAN *speaks.*

JUAN: Green she was, as green as a deep sea roller, and as beautiful as a ship in full sail – even her hair was green and long, right down her lovely back – but, lad, if ever anyone tells you they got a lovely singing voice – don't you believe 'em – Mieaau they does, just like an old tom cat. I tell ye . . .

TWO SAILORS *begin to taunt him.*

1ST SAILOR: What! that old fool! Spinning that yarn again? The old liar – mermaid? – what mermaid could he ever see? Why the old fool's so often drunk he can't tell a sprat from a . . .

JUAN (*in anger*): You shut that flapping mouth of yours. What should you know about a mermaid? I swear upon my mother's ring, 'twas green she was, and a beauty.

The ADMIRAL *enters, intent on navigational matters. He stands aloof.*

2ND SAILOR: Green she surely was – a stinking old cat-fish, green with age!

JUAN: Hell's rotten underside! You were both born liars afloat and worse ashore. She was a mermaid, did I not keep her in a barrel for all the world to see?

1ST
2ND SAILORS } : A cat-fish – a stinking, rotten . . .

JUAN *is quickly roused, and as the taunting continues, the* CREW *stops work and begins to crowd round: anything to break the routine . . .* JUAN *has soon had enough, and draws a knife with which to threaten the first sailor.*

The CAPTAIN *appears as the* BOS'N *pushes his way through the jeering crew. The* ADMIRAL *observes from a distance.*

CAPTAIN: Hold that man, take him below, bos'n, put him in chains; I'll have no fighting aboard ship.

ADMIRAL: By your leave, captain, I overheard the argument. This man is right, drunk or sober. It is permissible by the ship's law to catch a mermaid – how can we tell it is not mermaid's law to turn into a cat-fish, if caught by any other hands than merman's?

There is a growling laugh among the men; the CAPTAIN *signals to the Drummer-boy.*

CAPTAIN: Beat the starboard watch for'ard!

The DRUMMER-BOY *drums the crew away, while the* BOS'N *shouts orders.*

CAPTAIN: A mermaid! !

ADMIRAL: Yes, and a wondrous thing in his own mind, like an undiscovered land.

CAPTAIN: In yours? Sir, I must speak plain. You see the mood they are in?

ADMIRAL: You think the line is near, Captain?

CAPTAIN: The line, sir?

ADMIRAL: The line between man and beast, Captain.

CAPTAIN: If I and they are to stay this side the line, Admiral, then I must speak.

ADMIRAL: Say on.

CAPTAIN: Captain to Admiral – or man to man?

ADMIRAL: We are both men.

CAPTAIN: Then you are a fool. (*A pause.*)

ADMIRAL: Ah, a cutlass stroke!

CAPTAIN: 'Tis a sailor's weapon, for all it is English. A good plain edge, that bites to some effect, like my words to you, I hope. What is the effect of this direction? West, always west.

(*A drum is heard banging offstage and the stamp of running feet.*)

Never a turn to starboard, nor half a turn to port. For sixty-seven times that drum has rolled the evening watch,

c

with a bloody sun dead for'ard; and, when the bos'n shrills his morning pipe, there he is, dead aft, and that compass for all the change it has, might now be fixed in rust. That is why I have a surly crew, and why my officers each day use the rope's end more than the day before. The men are afraid, my Admiral, of drooping ship, sails cally cat and all over the sea's edge. Sir, I beg you, give my helmsman some other work to do.

ADMIRAL: They told me you were the best captain in all Spain.

CAPTAIN: I am.

ADMIRAL: Are you? Are you the man who knows the five seas like the back of his hand, the man who uses clouds for royals in any storm, can steal a capful of wind out of black fog? The man the English call the Spanish fox?

CAPTAIN: All Spain will tell you so.

ADMIRAL: Then would to God all Spain could see you now.

CAPTAIN: Sir, you go too far.

ADMIRAL: I have not gone far enough. Captain, the ship's boy, some of the men, might listen to that old man's tale; but some are men of reason. Why should the sun, the moon, and all those stars be rounded like a ball, yet not the earth? Look here, here, how can you stand here now upon this ship and find a bow of sea from north to south? And here, from east to west, and think the earth is like a biscuit floating in a bowl of milk? A flat thing, edged with space and water? Where is your sense, man?

CAPTAIN: So now I am a senseless one? I am no man of logic – just a plain sea captain.

ADMIRAL: Then 'Plain sea captain' . . .

CAPTAIN: And as that, Captain, I am responsible for the safety of my ship.

ADMIRAL: Your duty to me?

CAPTAIN: My duty to you, my ship, my crew are all one, sir; we have come far enough across the bow of sea. What do you hope to find? Some island full of pretty girls with priceless jewels in their hair?

ADMIRAL: Wait then, Captain. You say your duty is to your ship, your crew – I say this duty is more than that – it is to a nation – a world indeed, a world yet unborn, unthought of, yet as real as you or me. Where is your argument?

CAPTAIN: It is here, sir. I've listened to your theories but I do not agree. Every sailor worth the name well knows the world is flat. How could a sea stay on a rounded earth? What of the underside? Can a ship sail upside down? Can man or beast walk head down, feet up? No, 'tis flat, and therefore has an edge. The bargain I made with you was to sail to your directions, in a quest to find a short route to the Indies, within reasonable time. Now, with victuals low and water on scant ration, for these fifteen days a crew frightened to the edge of mutiny, yet each day still upon that blasted western course, I tell you that reasonable time is long past. Sir, will you give directions for a change of course?

ADMIRAL: No.

The lights fade, the spot again lights the OLD MARINER. *The* ADMIRAL *and* CAPTAIN *have disappeared.*

OLD MARINER: 'No! No!' he says – and, by the Lord, nothing will shake him from it. Now you see how it was, the captain wanting to go back, but the admiral determined to go on . . .

He is interrupted by the arrival of the three PINZON *brothers, striding in to dominate the scene. They are well-dressed, arrogant sea captains.*

MARTIN: Hold that, Seaman – what do you do here?

OLD MARINER: Captain Pinzon! Why, I was just telling these good people about the time when . . .

MARTIN: Yes, yes, I see who you are now. My brother and I stood awhile listening – and a fine lickspittle story you are making of it – be off with you now.

OLD MARINER: Ladies and Gentlemen, I . . .

MARTIN: Be off, I say, or by this hand . . .

The MARINER *leaves the arena.* CAPTAIN MARTIN *steps forward.*

MARTIN: Ladies and Gentlemen, may I introduce myself. My name is Martin Alonzo Pinzon, Captain of His Majesty's ship *Pinta* – my brothers, Francisco Martin, pilot of my ship and Vincente Yanez, Captain of the *Nina*. Quite a seagoing family, you may say. (*He laughs.*) As I said, we overheard this seaman fellow talking about the admiral of our little fleet. Bit of a sea-lawyer, that seaman, trouble-maker. Fortunately he is not serving aboard my ship; I have a very short way with sea-lawyers, short, but effective. I don't know how much this sailor told you, but I shouldn't like you to get the wrong impression about the admiral – I suppose he told you his name?

He is answered by two members of the audience.

FIRST PERSON: No, sir, we have not been told. The whole thing is a puzzle to me. Now you seem to be a man of some intelligence. Perhaps you would . . .

SECOND PERSON: Not so fast, not so fast. I've been a sailor myself. That old salt had only just begun his yarn, and I was very interested. It seemed to me he had something to say worth listening to.

FIRST PERSON: As I was about to ask, before your interruption. Will you . . . er . . .

MARTIN: Of course, of course, my dear sir. Well, to begin

with, the admiral's name is Cristforo Colombo, his ship the *Santa Maria*. My brothers and I are sailing with him and are endeavouring to find a shorter route to the Indies. This Colombo is a good enough sailor – of sorts, a fair maker of maps and charts. But, in my opinion, too much of a – a bit of a dreamer. Not as business-like as an admiral should be, certainly not man enough for that crew of his – half the sweepings of the Pimlos gaols – not man enough for the job.

VINCENTE: This is how I feel. Too quiet, too placid a man for a task like this, no dash; and yet, although my brother here has given financial aid to this expedition far in excess to that of Colombo, this man takes it upon himself to lead our little fleet.

MARTIN: Exactly, exactly, my dear Vincente. You'll see what I mean when I tell you he waited seven years at least before persuading his majesty, Ferdinand of Spain, that is of course partly, to help finance this journey; and it is my belief that if he had not gone to Queen Isabella cap in hand with some pitiful story or other . . .

FRANCISCO: Yet he has some good points.

Both CAPTAINS *turn upon him with anger.*

MARTIN ⎫
VINCENT ⎬ : Good points – ha!

SECOND PERSON (*in audience*): Go on, man, you speak – this chap must have some good points; we all have. You tell us your side of this man Colombo.

FRANCISCO *steps forward; his two brothers turn away in disdain.*

FRANCISCO: Well – all I wanted to say was, it seems to me that this Colombo has a great deal of tenacity in his character. I understand he has tramped all over Europe trying to find someone to take an interest in his idea of this short route to the Indies, before he came to Spain. Now we all know that money is a little short just now in Spain. The seven-year-war against the Moors has depleted the treasury chest, and the financial advisers of the Royal House are anxious to put gold into the coffers rather than take it out – and to them Colombo's expedition was a gamble; but the Queen was captivated by his idea, and she persuaded her husband that properly handled, it was a good investment.

Thunder rolls and the men look off anxiously.

FRANCISCO (*slyly to the audience*): Between you and me, that is also what my brother thought, and he became friendly with Colombo. My brother is no fool when it comes to making money.

Lightning flashes and then the thunder swells louder. Top lights fade.

VINCENTE: I must rejoin my ship – this will be a bad storm coming from the west.

MARTIN: Make ready the captain's boat there! Colombo has all sails set – is the man mad? The wind will rip the canvas to shreds. Look, look, how she rolls.

VINCENTE: Goodbye, brother. With regard to the matter discussed, I will not risk my ship upon this course after dawn breaks.

They salute each other and leave hastily as the BOS'N enters shouting orders to the crew.

The storm breaks on the arena and the action concentrates on the crew.

The Sea Chant (or Song) begins.

CREW: The sea! the sea! the sea! the sea!
Rolling starboard, league upon league,
League upon league, to port and aft,
For'ard,
And countless fathoms deep!

DRUMMER-BOY: Beat the drum! beat the drum!
  drum! drum! drum! drum!
  Beat the drum – beat the drum!
  Calling out the men.
  Beat the drum! beat the drum!
  Call the men to watch, lad,
  All the winds are . . .
CREW: The sea! the sea! the sea! the sea!
  Ever westward, crowding sail,
  Hauling sail to a lasting sky,
  And the endless, endless, endless sea!
DRUMMER-BOY: Beat the drum! beat the drum!
  Drum, drum, drum, drum,
  Beat the drum! beat the drum!
  Stormy sea and sky!
  Beat the drum! beat the drum!
  Sail's a'coming down, lads,
  Lash her up and make her fast
  And keep her snug and dry!
CREW: The sea! the sky! the sky! the sea!
  Never a hint of beast or bird!
  Lifting the hand to a straining eye!
  Look for dry, unmoving land.
DRUMMER-BOY: Beat the drum! beat the drum!
  drum, drum, drum, drum,
  Beat the drum! beat the drum!
  Every hand to sail!
  Beat the drum! beat the drum!
  Heave away my hearties!
  Bend your back, you laggards.
  Or you'll feel the bos'n's flail!

    The climax of the storm is reached, and the CREW *is sent
reeling and sprawling.*

1ST SAILOR: Mary, mother of Jesus, save me, a poor sailor from the edge of the world. Jesus, Son of God, save these sailors from the edge of the world! Turn the ship. Stop the wind! Make the sea dry up! But, oh God, Almighty God, save this ship from falling across the edge of the world!

The CREW *fall silent, watching him as he kneels at the foot of the rostrum.*

1ST SAILOR: Oh God, I am a vile sinner, we are all vile sinners. Yet I swear by the sweat of me face, by the rope-burns on me hands, by the pain in me guts, I'll be a good man – but, oh God, great God, wonderful God, save me and the rest of me mates from falling across the edge of the earth into the pit of everlasting fire.

Enter BOS'N.

BOS'N: Stow that, ye blabbering ape! Get up, ye hydra-headed web-footed seacat! Or by all that's holy I'll lay this rope across yer back!

1ST SAILOR: Beat me, then, lash me if you must! But I'll not put a hand to a rope until this ship changes course. Man, man, do you not see? Here is the world's end! Many a storm I've seen, but never a one like this. Look at them clouds, blacker than black they be, and piled as high as the devil's castle. Look at the waves; some so big they will smash this ship to a wreck in the flick of a knife! (*He draws his knife.*) Turn the ship, man, while you can. And run before the storm. (*Thunder rolls.*) Quick, man! Here is the world's edge!

BOS'N: I have no orders to . . .

The 1ST SAILOR *flings himself forward and has a knife at the Bos'n's throat. The* CREW *move in to help, roused by this action. The* CAPTAIN *appears. The crew face him, with the bos'n as hostage. The crew take their knives out.* COLOMBO *enters. The* CAPTAIN *appears against Colombo.*

COLOMBO: Release that man!

1ST SAILOR: Turn the ship before we will!

The CREW, *roused to action, call out loudly.*

CREW: Turn the ship! Change her course! The wheel! Sail east – sail east, etc. . . .

COLOMBO *(quietly)*: Release that man.

1ST SAILOR: I will kill him, if you do not change course!

COLOMBO: Kill him and we all die.

1ST SAILOR: How so?

COLOMBO: There are more of you than us. Kill him, and that is mutiny – and you must kill us. You will be alone on an uncharted sea. No one of you has sailed this far before. I know that no one of you has sailed more than three days out of sight of land. And those of you who 'volunteered' from the Pimlos gaol have never sailed before. How do you think you can find dry land – without our company?

CAPTAIN: Sir, they will release that man, and you will give me orders to turn about. I will navigate. To sail farther will endanger His Majesty's ship.

COLOMBO: You stand with the men against me?

CAPTAIN: Not against you, rather against unreason. This storm is a warning. I am not afraid of danger, but we are short of water and food. It will be a long journey home with more hazards than we bargained for.

COLOMBO: A longer journey than you bargained for. Captain, that log you hold is worthless. Two have been kept, one for yours and others' eyes – and the true log which I keep locked in an iron chest. Here is the key.

(Pause – COLOMBO *throws the key away.)*

We are much farther westward than you think, and only I know where you are.

*(*COLOMBO *turns away from them. The crew wait quietly*

*now for him to speak again. He is in no hurry, completely master
of the situation. He turns again.)*

Take my advice, gentlemen, don't be fools. By all the signs,
we are not far from land – new land. This morning we
heard strange noises – strange to your ears this far at sea.
It was the sound of birds' wings low on the water. At noon
the branch of a tree was floating off the starboard bow.

1ST SAILOR: Lies! lies! all lies! This is another of your tricks
– why did you not tell us about the birds? And why not
show us . . .

COLOMBO: Because, my friend, I hope to show you a far
nobler sight within a matter of hours – LAND, new undiscovered land! Does your heart not quicken with the thought
of it? You will have forged a new link between two mighty
countries. You will tread upon earth that the rest of the
world of men know nothing of. All your lives you will live
with a pride that nothing can tarnish. You will be rich,
honoured, respected. When your bones have crumbled to
dust, you will never be forgotten. Men will still talk of you
a thousand years from now, the handful of men and the
little ship that found the Indies. Will you throw all that
away for the idea of a fool? *(Points to first sailor.)* Will not
one of you stand firm?

*Silence. The DRUMMER-BOY suddenly heads from the crew
and stands with Colombo.*

DRUMMER-BOY: Here's one, my Admiral!

COLOMBO claps a hand on the boy's shoulder.

COLOMBO: So for'ard, lad, and watch.

(There is a cry from aloft.)

For'ard a light! a light for'ard, sir!

*All stand still and then move forward. Slowly the light grows.
A gun fires offstage. A sound of distant cheering.*

1ST SAILOR: The *Pinta*'s gun! That means . . .

COLOMBO: She has sighted . . .

(*A voice in a loud burst offstage.*)

LAND HO! LAND OFF THE FOR'ARD BOW, SIR! LAND
HO!

All SAILORS *stand grouped around* COLOMBO, *looking in
one direction. They begin to cheer as lights go down to blackout.*

The Chimney Sweeps

BY ANTHONY DELVES

CHARACTERS

WILLIAM BLAKE
THE BOY NED
HIS MOTHER AND FATHER
JACOB SHARP, MASTER SWEEP
ROSIE, HIS WIFE
RUFF, HIS SON
A PRIEST
TWO PAUPERS
SHINER, LEADER OF THE APPRENTICES

HUGH
RALPH
JOE
WILL   } *apprentice   sweeps*
TOM
PETE
FOOTMAN
BESSIE

THE CHIMNEY SWEEPS

Early morning in London, 1800. Perhaps a solitary bell, a cock crowing as the lights rise.

WILLIAM BLAKE *enters, carrying a large satchel with rolled prints obtruding; he wears an old cloak and hat. He stops, wipes his brow and gazes at the dawn on the horizon.*

BLAKE: 'The sun arises in the East
    Clothed in robes of blood and gold'
Yes, robes of blood and gold. The city is dressed in the fine garments of the sun and I see blood and gold. Their other names are suffering and poverty.

(He puts down his large satchel, and slips off his cloak.)
I remember this walled walk when it was a green with children playing beneath the trees. Now they must go to Vauxhall Gardens and promenade through the Grove, or stay here in backstreets and alleyways. This parish of Lambeth sickens and languishes. Sixteen almshouses we boast of; would they were all closed and the Philanthropic Society dead! Where is the Lamb in Lambeth? The Lamb of Innocence!

The sound of running and cries is followed by the entrance of a BOY, *exhausted and dishevelled, poorly dressed. He looks desperately at Blake, who impulsively beckons the boy to hide by his satchel.* BLAKE *covers him with his cloak.*

Enter the master-sweep, JACOB SHARP, *and his son,* RUFF. *The runaway's* MOTHER *and* FATHER *follow them and stand at side.* SHARP *stops in his tracks, uncertain which direction to take.*

SHARP: Excuse me, sir, but did you notice a little ruffian run this way just now?

BLAKE *looks up casually.*

BLAKE: If you mean a mite standing but four foot in his shoes, with hair like a mongrel's matted coat, complexion like mud at the bottom of the river, and generally in need of a good meal – I must reply 'Yes'. But why are you hunting the child? Has he wronged you?

SHARP: Indeed he has! This gentle lady here, sir, this morning concluded a bargain, I should say a contract, with me, sir.... I am, sir, your obedient acquaintance, Jacob Sharp, chimney sweeper of distinction.

BLAKE (*returning the compliment coldly*): William Blake, painter, poet, and of distinction.

RUFF, *Sharp's son, has been eyeing Blake and his cloak. He prods the cloak, and now with a yelp of triumph pulls it from the boy who lies huddled on the ground.* SHARP *growls his satisfaction and begins to advance on the boy.* BLAKE *pulls him back, and a* PRIEST *enters in time to intervene.*

BLAKE: Stand your distance, Sharp. Touch the boy, and I'll mark *you* for good.

PRIEST (*intervening*): Restrain yourself, Jacob Sharp. There is no need for violence. (*To Sharp, quietly.*) This is Blake – William Blake. They say he's half mad. Not so long ago he almost murdered a man for approaching his wife. Let him alone.

SHARP: He may be his gracious majesty King George for all I care. The law's on my side!

PRIEST: To whom does the boy belong?

SHARP (*with venom*): Me! I have him as an apprentice, see, by arrangement with his mother and father; but, before we had finished the business, the brat ran off, and we found him with this man here. (*He flourishes a piece of paper.*)

BLAKE: Business you call it! Prisons are built with stones of law. How much did you pay them for the child?

SHARP (*blustering*): Pay them? What, *me* pay *them*? Let me tell you, I'm a master-sweep and an honest man.

PRIEST (*who has examined the contract card handed to him*): This contract seems in order. Why are you causing trouble again, Master Blake?

FATHER (*approaching Blake*): What has it to do with you? You're not a gentleman. We don't mean our son any harm. We've just found him work, and God knows that's hard enough to find. There will be more for his brothers now.

MOTHER: And his sisters – poor little mites. It's God's will.

BLAKE (*exasperated*): Expect poison from standing water! (*To Sharp.*) Have you not enough apprentices from the workhouse?

SHARP: No. They are being filched by the factories in the north. Don't blame me. They go off in batches – even the idiot-children are taken. There's precious little for the likes of me.

MOTHER: At least our Ned is not going far away.

SHARP: Go to the market in Bethnal Green on a Monday or Tuesday morning, you'll see them all lined up for hire. I'm doing these two fond parents a favour, I am.

PRIEST: There is nothing you can do, Blake. Nor is there anything you *should* do. A sweep's work is good labour – and the child will be kept from idleness and corruption.

SHARP: So I'll bid you good day, Master Blake. Perhaps I'll see you again while I and my apprentices are about our lawful business. I hope you'll keep to yours. Good day, Father (*to Priest*) and don't worry about little Ned. (*To Parents.*) I'll look after him. Come on, Ned, little chap – here, have a lump of sugar. (*He takes it from his waistcoat. Ned is hungry and takes it.*) Here, Ruff (*to his son*),

D

hold Ned's hand nicely now – see he doesn't make a bolt for it.

MOTHER (*sobbing*): God bless you, son. (*She goes to Ned and hugs him briefly.*)

FATHER (*weakly*): Be a good lad, now, Ned. (NED *stifles his tears and leaves, held firmly by Ruff.*)

    SHARP, RUFF *and* NED *exeunt.* MOTHER *and* FATHER *wave goodbye and then leave, the mother still sobbing.*

BLAKE (*slow and deliberate*): Why? Why? He will be little better than a slave.

PRIEST (*quickly*): So are we all, Blake, slaves to sin.

BLAKE: An innocent child!

PRIEST: It is the Lord's will, as well as his parents. Heaven has provided, and it is our duty to accept . . .

BLAKE: Heaven! This is Man's providence, not God's! (*Angry.*) Better to steal and destroy than to countenance such slavery.

PRIEST: You go against the Church's teachings, Blake. You know your ten commandments.

BLAKE (*furious*): Then we must break the commandments! I tell you Jesus acted from impulse, not from rules and laws.

PRIEST (*coldly*): And I tell you, Master William Blake, that you are an ignorant man and had better stay at your printing press. I bid you good day.

    (PRIEST *exit. Enter two young* PAUPERS.)

BLAKE (*shouting after Priest*): And I bid you heed the voice of the angels, you priest of the raven with your black wings and your croaking carping. You deny your Maker. For everything that lives is holy . . . (*He notices the two* PAUPERS, *one of whom stares vacantly at him, the other ferrets around on the ground.*)

BLAKE: . . . however lowly. You, sir, what are you doing?

(*The first* PAUPER *looks up. He is quite chirpy despite his appearance. A tin whistle hangs from his neck.*)

1ST PAUPER: Me, sir? I'm making a collection in my little bag.

BLAKE: What are you collecting?

1ST PAUPER (*grinning*): Droppings, sir . . . you know, from dogs and horses.

2ND PAUPER: Turds. (*He is half-witted.*)

BLAKE: And what do you do with them?

1ST PAUPER: We sell 'em, to the tanneries. A bagful fetches a tidy price.

BLAKE: Is there no other work for you?

1ST PAUPER: Well, I used to sweep, sir, but . . . Sam here was in the match factory.

BLAKE: Isn't that better than doing this?

1ST PAUPER: Well, now that depends . . . I mean, look at Sam. What's that yellow on your jaw, Sam?

2ND PAUPER: Prosperous.

1ST PAUPER: Phosphorus. It's eating his jaw away – that's what you get making matches. That, and the smell.

BLAKE: And you, you were a sweep once?

1ST PAUPER: Yes, those were good days. I was serving a regular apprenticeship – seven years. We had some fun, all the lads, and sometimes we'd make tuppence or threepence a day – a tanner at a big house. It's a knack, is climbing. (*He sits, gnawing at an apple core, and warms to his reminiscence.*) You see, there are two or three ways of climbing up the chimneys. In the wide flues, you climb with elbows and legs spread out, your feet pressing against the sides of the flues. But in the narrow ones, such as nine-inch wide ones, you must slant it – get your sides in the angles because it's wider there and go up that way, like this. (*He starts to demonstrate the climbing, twisting action.*) There, that's 'slanting'. I never got stuck myself.

BLAKE: But some did?

1ST PAUPER: Only two in four years. Two mates. Choked, they were. They had to knock half a chimney down to get one out. But I was all right. Till I fell off a roof. See this arm? Well, it won't bend, see? Funny, isn't it? So no more climbing for me. I don't mind doing this turd-collecting – it's better than starving, mate. Here, Sam . . .

(*During this account,* 2ND PAUPER *has edged round to sit by Blake's satchel and has furtively extracted foodstuffs and pocketed them. He is caught in the act by* 1ST PAUPER, *who breaks his speech to Blake.*)

. . . put that back, don't rob *him.*

BLAKE (*smiling*): Don't worry. Here, Sam, have one of these. (*Offers a print, which he partly unrolls.*) You can keep it.

2ND PAUPER (*scowling*): Don't want it!

BLAKE: Nor does anyone else, it seems. Yet I tell you these drawings were made with the help of angels. If you want to know what an angel looks like, look at this. (2ND PAUPER *backs away.*) No, the world does not want to know. But come, both of you, I have some cheese and bread in my satchel, and there is water near my house. Lead on, piper, pipe us down the valley.

He shoulders his satchel, and they leave, with the first pauper playing his tin whistle.

Enter JACOB, *cursing and threatening,* RUFF *grinning and* NED *crying.*

SHARP (*throwing Ned to ground*): Stay here, you little cur! Move an inch and as sure as Gawd made little apples, I'll strike you down. (*To Ruff.*) Come on, Ruff, 'elp me unlock the others. (*Shouting to wife.*) Rosie!

ROSIE (*offstage*): 'Allo?

SHARP: Bring out the food, will yer?

ROSIE: Right.

> SHARP *and* RUFF *leave* NED *sobbing on floor. A shed door is heard being opened offstage.*

SHARP (*offstage*): Gid up, yer layabouts! Come out of it! Gid out and get some food quick. Hurry up, Rosie, we're late enough already.

ROSIE (*offstage*): All right, all right, stop moaning!

> *Four dirty, shabbily-dressed and hungry-looking* BOYS *appear, stretching themselves. They carry stools, bowls and spoons.* NED *looks up and stops snivelling. He is noticed by the boys. One of them, their leader, speaks first.*

SHINER: New, ain't yer? (NED *nods his head.*) Ever swept before? (NED *shakes his head.*)

PETE: You got a tongue, mate?

NED (*nods and then adds*): Yes.

SHINER (*looking at him more closely*): You been crying, ain't yer? Eh? Why?

> (NED *shows the red marks across his legs.*)

Cor! That ain't nothing, mate. You wanna see 'im after he's been on the bottle!

> *The others nod agreement. Two more* BOYS *enter, followed by* JACOB, RUFF, *and* ROSIE *with the food. The* BOYS *perk up excitedly at the sight of the food.*

SHARP: Gid down! Gid down! Wait for it, then! Remember your table manners.

> SHARP *grins broadly and takes a hunk of meat from* ROSIE; *he holds it above one of the boys,* SHINER.

SHARP: Look what I've found then, Shiner. A nice tasty slice of lamb. You wouldn't be a-fancying *that*, would you?

> *He dangles it above* SHINER, *who with the others looks at it hungrily.* SHINER *reaches for it.* SHARP *laughs and holds it higher.*

SHARP: Come on then, Shiner. Up, boy! Come on, I'll tire of your fickleness in a minute.

    SHINER *reaches as high as he can.* SHARP *puts the meat in his hands and* SHINER *bites at it. The other boys surge forward but* SHARP *snarls at them.*

SHARP: Back you go! Sit up! (*He takes the bread from Rosie and throws it in the middle of the boys. They scramble and fight each other for a bit. The* SHARPS *look on with indifference.* ROSIE *now places two filthy, black saucepans down, one containing water, the other porridge. The* BOYS *huddle round these, while the Sharps talk.*)

ROSIE: So yer got the new 'un all right, Jay. (*She doles out porridge.*)

SHARP: Yeah! I had a tip-off. I 'ad to pay half a crown for 'im, though.

ROSIE: 'Alf a bleeding crown! They goes up in price – up and up – and gets worser an' worser in quality. Time was when the best went for no more than a shilling an' ninepence!

RUFF (*nibbling at some bread*): Times change, Ma.

ROSIE (*seeing him nibbling*): 'Ere put that down! Do you want make yourself sick?

RUFF: That lot 'ave it, and it don't do them much harm.

ROSIE: Them's vermin, and vermin can stomach it. Besides your meal's ready by now. (*Serving the last boy.*)

RUFF: Well, I'm hungry, Ma.

ROSIE: Well, come on then. You and your father. (RUFF *exit.*)

SHARP: Right-o, love. (*To boys.*) Shiner, I leave you in charge. Any trouble an' I'll 'ave yer – cor Christ, I will . . . (*Exit.*)

ROSIE: And mind you wash them bowls this time! (*Exit.*)

    The boys are sitting on stools in a circle eating porridge. NED *tries his gingerly. They are on their own.*

SHINER (*to Ned*): What you called, mate?

NED: Ned.

SHINER: Ned what?

NED (*after thinking*): I don't know.

SHINER: Ned 'I don't know'! Blimey, that's a funny name, i'n it? (*The others titter.*) Been up a chimney before, then, 'ave yer?

NED: No, never . . . is it, is it very awful?

WILL: Christ! you're telling me. You'll 'ave your first try today, to see 'ow fast you is, and tonight Mrs Rosie'll give yer the first scrubbing.

NED: Tonight! Scrubbing?

SHINER: 'Ere, look at me knees and me elbows – go on, feel 'em! they don't bite. Well?

NED: They – they're very 'ard.

SHINER: An' I should say so too! Old Rosie scrubbed them for months, and when they's clean they's shiney – so that's how I'm Shiner!

NED (*brief laugh*): Oh! (*Brief pause.*) What's scrubbing?

SHINER: Well, look 'ere, the flesh must be 'ardened, see? And so it has to be rubbed 'ere on the elbows and on the knees in perticuler. Old Mrs Rosie'll do it by 'er fire with strong brine, see, and he'll stand over you with a cane, and coax yer with an half-penny to stand a few more rubs. If yer scream too much, he'll strike yer round the gob, and Ruff will come an' punch yer.

NED: It must be very painful.

HUGH: Christ! it's worse than getting stuck in them chimneys – but we've all 'ad it done some time or other.

SHINER: At first you'll come back from the chimneys with yer arms and knees streaming with blood.

JOE: And yer knees look as if the caps had been pulled off, and the . . .

SHINER: Then they must be rubbed with brine again, and on the raw flesh . . . the agony!

HUGH: Makes me shudder to think o' it, the pains rip through your body like Christ knows what. (*With consolation.*) You'll smile again though, mate.

NED (*attempts a smile*): And the climbing?

HUGH: Just as bad, mate . . . just as bad.

SHINER: The climbing's all right.

RALPH: It's like going up a long black box.

JOE: You press yourself against the side, see, and heave up and up.

TOM: But the soot clogs your eyes, and you swallow it.

HUGH: It stifles yer throat.

SHINER: You heave up and up, brushing as you go, praying for the top.

RALPH: But prayers don't do much good these days.

    The boys momentarily depressed.

HUGH: God don't care about us – only them rich ones that gives him money.

NED: What . . . what if you won't climb?

SHINER(*fiercely*): He'll whip yer and flog yer till you're crying to get up the chimney.

    The BOYS *begin to 'persecute' Ned, eventually advancing round him and at the climax of the 'attack' they rattle their spoons in the bowls they carry over the crouching Ned.*

HUGH: And if you are just a little way up, he'll stick pins in yer feet to make yer climb.

JOE: Or light straw beneath yer.

RALPH: The lighted straw soon chokes yer tubes.

WILL: Gawd! You fight to get up, fight to get down, anything to breathe again.

TOM: And the flue goes up twisting and turning, cutting your sides and choking your throat. (*He demonstrates.*)

SHINER: You're caught in a bend . . .

PETE: You wriggle and pull . . .

HUGH: And shout and scream . . .

SHINER: But there's nothing but black soot to hear you . . .

RALPH: Your eyes grow heavier and heavier . . .

TOM: Slowly, slowly the soot clogs your throat . . .

SHINER: To swallow would be 'eaven itself . . .

PETE: The noise of 'im cursing and swearing below gets fainter and fainter.

JOE: As your heart beats faster, and faster, and faster.

> *The* BOYS *rattle the spoons in their bowls till* NED *cries out, and they jeer and laugh; at length they calm down and return to their stools. One boy,* RALPH, *kneels by Ned, and part of the poem by William Blake forms their dialogue.*

RALPH: Where are thy father and mother? Say?

NED: They are both gone up to the church to pray;
Because I was happy upon the heath
And smiled among the winter's snow,
They clothed me in the clothes of death
And taught me to sing the notes of woe
And because I am happy and dance and sing
They think they have done me no injury
And are gone to praise God and his priest and king
Who make up a Heaven of our misery.

RALPH: Gone to praise God and his priest and king

JOE: Who make up a Heaven of our misery.

PETE (*quieter*): On a Sunday morning you can 'ear 'em all chanting their prayers and (*mimicking*) 'Praise be to Jesus'.

HUGH: Them priests ain't so holy neither – times I've seen them rolling – stuck as pigs – ain't no one's business.

RALPH: I told that vicar that Sharp 'ad pinched me from me parents, an' he just smirked and told me to be thankful for a bit of work.

SHINER: They're rotten, the whole ruddy lot of 'em.
    Slight pause.

JOE: Back 'ome I knew a vicar an' he was all right – 'e used to
    let us 'ave con . . . conf . . .

WILL: Confessions!

JOE: Yeah, confessions – cheap rate, and sometimes 'e gave
    us a farthing.

WILL: My vicar told me that there was angels in the skies with
    big white wings.

TOM: An' they 'elp you when you're in a bit of trouble.

WILL: He said they're buzzing all round yer head 'cos God's
    told 'em to keep us good.

JOE (*smaller and even more innocent than the rest*): When you see
    them sea-gulls squawking up in the sky, they ain't really
    sea-gulls – they're messengers to the angels, from God,
    that's why they're white.

RALPH: Yeah, that's what my mum said too.

HUGH (*with more interest*): Is God really the nice gentleman they
    say 'e is?

SHINER: He ain't done much for us, 'as he?

TOM: I still think he's up there, though . . .

RALPH: Perhaps he's asleep.

JOE: My mum said he's all right – she speaks to 'im.

WILL: He . . . he . . . shows me the angels every night. (*The
    others take interest.*)

HUGH: What do they say, Will?

WILL: They say, 'Never mind, Will, we're with you. Be a
    good boy and you'll go to heaven'.

SHINER: Did . . . did they say anything about the rest of us?

WILL: Oh yes, they said God wants us all and really *does* love
    us. We'll play on the green grass again, laugh in the sun,
    God will be watching, keeping us from trouble.

TOM: Tell us, Will. Tell us *all* what the angels said.

WILL: 'When my mother died I was very young,
And my father sold me while yet my tongue
Could scarcely cry "Weep! Weep! Weep! Weep!"
So your chimneys I sweep and in your soot I sleep.
(*He goes to 2nd boy, Tom.*)
There's little Tom Dacre who cried when his head
That curled like a lamb's back, was shaved, so he said,'
TOM: 'Hush, Tom, never mind it, for when your head's bare
You know that the soot cannot spoil your white hair.
And so I was quiet.'
WILL: 'And that very night
As Tom was sleeping he had such a sight!
That thousands of sweepers, Dick, Joe, Ned, Jack,
Were all of them locked in coffins of black.'
TOM: 'And by came an angel who had a bright key,
And he opened the coffins and set them all free.
Then down a green plain, leaping, laughing, they run
And wash in a river and shine in the sun.
Then naked and white, all their bags left behind,
They rise upon clouds and sport in the wind.'
  TOM *has risen, his eyes shining.*
WILL (*excited*): 'And the angel told Tom, if he'd be a good boy,
He'd have God for his father and never want joy.'
JOE (*repeating*): 'He'd have God for a father . . .'
PETE: Tell us again, little Tom! (*All the boys have jumped up
and as* TOM *speaks again, they take up the words and dance round
in crazy jubilation shouting 'leaping', 'laughing', 'wash in a
river', 'shine in the sun'.*)
TOM: 'Down a green plain leaping, laughing, they run, and
wash in a river and shine in the sun . . .' . . . 'they rise upon
clouds, and sport in the wind . . .'
  The noise is now so loud that SHARP *enters, followed by*
RUFF *who is still eating. The* BOYS *suddenly stop.*

SHARP (*astounded*): Shiner, what 'ave you lot been up to?

SHINER: Nothing, sir, nothing! We were just . . . dreaming.

SHARP: Well, when you've finished your beauty sleep, there's work to be done. Set to, you lot. Bags and brushes, hurry up. And you two (*indicates two boys*), fetch the cart (*they go*). And you, young Ned, come here. (NED *retreats, but* RUFF *grabs his arm.*) I'll learn you. We'll have none of your runaway tricks!

(*The cart is brought in, and* SHARP *manacles Ned to it by one arm.*)

We'll keep you under personal supervision, we will. And you can learn a thing or two about the craft of sweeping today. All right, lads? Everyone ready? (*All the boys gather round to push and pull the cart;* SHARP *mounts it.*) Rosie, love! We're off – over to Lambeth market-place.

ROSIE (*appearing*): All right, Jacob. Have a good day. Don't be late back. I'm going down to the market for some nice pig's trotters this morning.

SHARP: There'll be a drop of Geneva with them this evening, dearie. Come on then, get shoving, you lot. Ruff, give us a tune to help us on our way.

RUFF *has a pipe, or drum, and he sets them off. The boys take the cart round the arena, whistling and singing, more from habit than pleasure.* NED *is pulled along.*

Enter BLAKE *with the two* PAUPERS *following.* BLAKE *advances indignantly. The cart is stopped.*

BLAKE: Why is the boy chained up?

SHARP (*surly*): He's a security risk, this one! I can't trust him at liberty so I have to lock him up.

BLAKE: Surely their plight is hard enough without treating them as animals? Man, have you no heart? Have you no conscience?

SHARP: I don't know what you're talking about, mister. No heart? No conscience? You're balmy, that's your trouble.

BLAKE: Look at this spectacle, friends. (*He addresses the two Paupers.*) Every child a ruined human wretch – a vermin-ridden parasite – God's forgotten race. In misery they breathe and in misery they shall expire.

1ST PAUPER: I dunno, mate, they don't look too bad to me. I'd rather sweep chimneys than starve.

SHINER (*indignant*): Watch it, mister, we're not dead yet!

SHARP: Be off with you, crackpot poet. Get out of our way!

BLAKE: Not till you release that boy from chains of servitude!

Enter ROSIE *with a liveried* FOOTMAN.

ROSIE: Cor, here's good fortune! The cart's been held up on the road. Jacob, I've been chasing you round the streets. This is Lord Longford's gentleman-attendant. He's got orders for you; he nearly came too late.

FOOTMAN (*aloof but rather out of breath*): Master Jacob Sharp? I 'ave 'ere an urgent communication from his Lordship's bailiff, and I'm to accompany you at once to the house.

He hands a letter to SHARP, *who opens it, can't read, and gives it to Rosie as he descends from cart. There now ensues a double conversation as* BLAKE *draws* FOOTMAN *aside. The boys settle back to wait.*

BLAKE (*to Footman*): Listen! Can you stand by and see innocence destroyed by such oppression? Do you see that child there?

ROSIE (*reading*): Let's see what his Lordship says. Ooh *all* the chimneys of the Manor House, Jacob, fifty-three chimneys!

FOOTMAN (*to Blake*): What's wrong, eh?

SHARP: Fifty-three? Let's see.

BLAKE (*to Footman*): That unhappy boy is chained, a lamb to the slaughter!

ROSIE (*reads*): '. . . herewith demands that the rooms be ready for his home-coming

FOOTMAN(*mystified*): Slaughter? Here, what's going on?

BLAKE: I want you to help me get him released from slavery.

FOOTMAN: Isn't he an apprentice?

BLAKE: If he is, he shouldn't be chained up. (*He advances on Sharp.*) Jacob Sharp, you have no right to . . .

and all chimneys thoroughly cleaned . . .'

SHARP: Rosie, this is a great opportunity. The best bit of luck for months. I'll have all my lads up the fifty-three in no time. Come on! Hey!

He starts to mount cart.

SHARP: No right! and who are you to tell me right or wrong. (*To Footman.*) I don't know what he's been telling you, my friend, but he's mad enough for Bedlam. Out of my way, I've work to do.

BLAKE (*snatching a shovel from cart*): Then I'll give you proof of my sanity! (*He threatens Sharp.*)

SHARP (*humouring the madman*): All right, all right, William Blake. No need to go wild. Look, you don't like this lad being chained up – well, he's dangerous. When people are dangerous they get chained up. He's not like these others – they're happy, hardworking 'prentices. Aren't they, Ruff?

RUFF: That's right, Dad, always singin' and dancin'.

SHARP (*eyes still on Blake*): Rosie, my dear, you tell Master Blake about the Sweeps' Dance last May Day.

ROSIE: Well, they have a day off first of May. And they collect money in the streets – for themselves, of course; we don't touch nothing. (*Sharp cuffs one would-be protester.*) They all dress up, the young sweeps do, red faces and leaves all over them. And they dance, see. There's one that's dressed as a Lady – it was Joe here last time, lovely Lady he made – (*Joe is thrust forward*) and Will was the Lord (RUFF *shoves Will forward*); the other lads make a tune and beat time

with their brushes and shovels while they dance. It's ever
so gay and 'appy.

SHARP (*aware that Blake's anger is subsiding*): Now, if you give
that shovel to Shiner there, the lads will show you what I
mean. Here, Shiner, show the gentleman your dance – go
on, and it's a tot of gin for you tonight. (SHINER *shrugs,
takes the shovel that now hangs loosely from Blake's hand, gets
the boys in line.*) Come on, you lot, dance!

RUFF *plays the tune on his pipe and the* BOYS *go through the
Dance sequence, sulkily at first but as the tune livens they respond.
The audience of* SHARP, ROSIE, FOOTMAN *and two*
PAUPERS *enjoy the show but* BLAKE *has had enough. He breaks
through the line of dancers, almost incoherent as he shouts at
Sharp.*

BLAKE: Enough! The terrible smitings of Luvah crushing the
body of Albion. The voice of Urizen thundering all around.
I have a vision of your damnation, Jacob Sharp! Flames of
sulphurous fire roar round you, I hear you groan, swallowed
in a horrible din in agony on agony. Through the confusion,
like a crack across from immense to immense, loud, strong,
a universal groan of death, louder than all the wracking
elements, deafen'd and rended worse than Urizen . . .

*He is held by Footman, the two Paupers, then the boys and
hurled out shouting, accompanied by the Paupers.*

SHARP: I don't know who he is but he's mad.

ROSIE: Never mind about him, Jacob. Get down to Longford
House.

SHARP: You're right, Rosie, my dear. Come on, you lot. And
as for you (*to Ned, with a cuff*), take that for causing the
delay! Get pulling! Forward! Follow that gentleman and
we are on the way to Lord Longford's estate . . . and we're
going up fifty-three chimneys, me lads, fifty-three!

The cart is pulled round the arena as the BOYS *whistle to*

Ruff's tune. The FOOTMAN *marches ahead. As they approach the House, the* BOYS *begin to look up at the high walls and chimneys and their whistling ceases.*

FOOTMAN: Here we are, then, his Lordship's Manor House. Most of it built in Henry the Eighth's time, with a new south front on other side from here. The bailiff's out riding this morning, and my orders are to get you started. So, when you are ready, Master Sharp.

SHARP (*impressed by the House*): Delighted, my old friend. At your service. At once, no delay. (*He dismounts.*) Shiner! Do your usual. Take the lads and give them a chimney each. Plenty of bags in the cart. I'll be inside in a jiffy. Go on, then, all of you. Move!

   SHINER *gives orders,* BOYS *take brushes, shovels and bags. They go out, leaving Ned still chained and* SHARP *taking a flask from his pocket.*

SHARP (*swigging*): A very nice property, my old friend (*to Footman*), and a lovely collection of old chimneys, I'll be bound. When is his Lordship returning to the House?

FOOTMAN: That, Master Sharp, is no concern of yours. Do you wish to inspect the chimneys with me now?

   Enter BESSIE, *a maid from the kitchens.*

BESSIE: Here, Nicholas, are you leaving all that silver about with these sweep boys sculling about the buttery?

FOOTMAN (*worried*): I must go, can't trust anyone these days. I don't suppose it would ever occur to you, Bessie, to put the silver away yourself! (*He goes out.*)

SHARP (*slowly*): Bessie Cooper! If it isn't Bessie Cooper! Thought you'd gone over the waters, old dear. What are you doing here, you old honey-bag!

BESSIE: Keep a still tongue, Jacob Sharp. Ask no questions and you'll not get told any lies. Never mind how I got away nor how I got employment here. I shan't be here

much longer either. Listen, I knew you were sent for . . .
(*Suddenly she notices Ned by the cart.*) What's he doing there?

SHARP: Never mind him. He's a new 'prentice. Cost me half
a crown, and all he can do is blub.

BESSIE: He can blab, too. Send him away.

SHARP: Not likely! I don't want no runaway on my hands.

BESSIE: Well, what I have to say is not for his ears. Come over
here. (SHARP *moves over but before she can speak* SHINER *returns.*)

SHINER: Hey, Mr Sharp, aren't you coming in? I've set the
boys up the chimneys in the big rooms, but there's a small
fireplace in the Lord's study, there's books over all the walls.
I can't get any of the lads to go up that flue.

SHARP (*impatiently*): What d'you mean, 'can't'? Shove Joe
up, he's small enough!

SHINER: He won't get far, it's a twister, is that one. And he's
gone up the chimney in the dining hall now.

BESSIE: Send him. (*She indicates Ned.*)

SHARP: What, him? Why not, he's built for small flues. Give
the brat his first sweep.

NED: No, don't send me, I don't know what to do!

SHARP (*unlocking Ned*): Give him your brush and bag, Shiner.
Send him up. And if you have any trouble stick a few pins
in his feet, or light that bag of straw. (*He takes sack from cart.*)
And tell Ruff to get out of the kitchen and help push him
up. Come on, you slippery eel, get on with the work! (NED
is taken out by SHINER, *leaving* SHARP *alone with* BESSIE.)
Now, come on, Bessie, out with it. What are you plotting?

BESSIE: You haven't changed your ways, Jacob! Still game
for a quick fortune the wrong side of the law?

SHARP: You can trust me, Bessie. I took one look at this place
and knew there was a treasure-house here. Now, if you are
on the inside and want a little help, you can count on your
old friend Jacob Sharp.

E

BESSIE: Say no more. Now listen, his Lordship returns next Sunday. The whole house is being done over – we're all slaving to get everything clean . . . and that includes the family plate. You should see it! Gold and silver – dishes and goblets! And I've got the key . . .!

    RUFF *interrupts, running in.*

RUFF: Dad, that new 'un's got stuck in the second bend.

SHARP (*not listening*): Keep quiet, son. Go on, Bessie.

RUFF: But, Dad, he can't move! And he's hollering . . .

SHARP (*cuffing Ruff*): Get back in. Tell Shiner to poke him out. Go on! (RUFF *reluctantly runs out.*)

BESSIE (*returning to Sharp's side*): I want someone I can trust with a cart.

SHARP: Ah, it'll be a tidy haul then. And . . .?

BESSIE: Yes!

SHARP: You know me, Bessie. Always game to help a friend.

BESSIE: Well, this evening then. But we've to move quickly. Now Nicholas always leave the Buttery unlocked at . . .

    SHINER *rushes in terrified.*

SHINER: He's stuck, proper stuck. Can't get to him!

SHARP: Now what is it? Who's stuck?

SHINER: Ned, the new one. That flue's only nine inches. I made him climb up but he's stuck!

SHARP: Gawd, what I have to put up with! Can't you find another flue to him?

    FOOTMAN *enters.*

SHINER: There isn't one till two floors up.

FOOTMAN (*anxious*): All this noise echoing round the house! What about that boy up the chimney in the library?

SHARP: Now don't you start! I'm just coming. Bessie, don't go away, you haven't said what time.

    BOYS *rush in panic-stricken.* FOOTMAN *exits.*

TOM: He's stopped crying, sir! In fact he ain't making no noise at all now.

SHARP: Well, why the plague didn't you go and pull him down? *He is still torn between Bessie and the tragedy.*

TOM (*crying*): Because he's probably dead and, if he fell on me, we'd both be gonners, wouldn't we?

Sudden noise and shouts. FOOTMAN *enters.*

FOOTMAN (*pale*): He's fallen – he must have stifled up there!

SHARP (*suddenly realizing*): Fallen! What's happened? Why can't you lads get on with a job when it's . . .

He stops as Ned's body is brought in and laid by the boys on the cart.

SHARP: It's the fault of them chimneys! Them old ones is too narrow. They shouldn't expect to have them swept, much too dangerous. (BESSIE *begins to leave.*) Here, Bessie, wait a minute. I've got a bit of trouble here.

BESSIE: I can see that. No good, Jacob, not now, you've got your hands full – and your cart. (*She leaves.*)

SHARP: Bessie! You can trust me . . . (*Notices all standing dumbly looking at him.*) This will take some explaining, this will. Here, old friend (*to Footman*), don't forget I was there with that boy helping him when he had – a heart-attack.

FOOTMAN: Well, I can hardly say that, with Lord Longford coming home so soon . . .

SHARP (*hastily finding sovereigns to give footman*): Maybe this will give you a better memory. We don't want no trouble, eh? I'll take the lad away and no more said.

FOOTMAN: You'd better leave at once. I'll tell the bailiff you couldn't complete the work.

SHARP: Yes, that's so. (*Turns to boys around cart.*) And listen, Shiner and the rest of you, that poor boy had a weak heart and that's why it happened. If one of you so much as breathe anything else, I'll flay you alive.

SHINER: But . . .

SHARP: Keep your mouth shut, all of you! Now keep quiet, put the gear on the cart and let's get back home.

The BOYS *pack up and form up to pull the cart.* RUFF *starts to play a tune, but* SHINER *thumps him.* RUFF *tries to protest, but* SHARP *does nothing. They march round the arena silently.* SHARP *brings up the rear slowly, wearing his hat. The* FOOTMAN *leaves. Church bells ring out dolefully. As they process, they pass in succession the* PRIEST, *who prays quietly – and* SHARP *removes his hat. The two* PAUPERS, *who simply stare blankly, the* MOTHER *and* FATHER, *who sob quietly together, and then* WILLIAM BLAKE.

A single bell tolls. The cart is pulled off. JACOB SHARP *sees Blake standing there, stops and then defiantly puts his hat on. He follows the cart.*

BLAKE *is left to look after them.*

BLAKE: I wander thro' each charter'd street,
Near where the charter'd Thames does flow,
And mark in every face I meet
Marks of weakness, marks of woe.

In every cry of every Man,
In every Infant's cry of fear,
In every voice, in every ban,
The mind-forg'd manacles I hear.

How the Chimney sweeper's cry
Every black'ning Church appals;
And the hapless Soldier's sigh
Runs in blood down Palace walls

And before the poem ends BLAKE *has walked out of the arena as the light fades.*

The Tale
of the Four Winds

A Fantasy in the Chinese Manner

BY MICHAEL MORLEY

CHARACTERS

NORTH WIND (*male*)
SOUTH WIND (*male*)
EAST WIND (*female*)
WEST WIND (*female*)

SPIRITS OF THE FOUR WINDS (*front rows of audience*)

THE EMPEROR
SHANTI-LO (*Plenipotentiary extraordinary*)
NANTING-HI (*Prime Minister*)
THE CHIEF JUSTICE
THE COURT JESTER
EXECUTIONER
SERVANT
THE EMPRESS
THE OLD HERMIT OF THE HILLS
THE KITCHEN-BOY (*the Hero*)
THE PRINCESS OF THE MOUNTAIN PEOPLE (*the Heroine*)
HER TWO LADIES-IN-WAITING (*dancers, who also play the part of* TWO VULTURES)
RETINUE OF MOUNTAIN PEOPLE (*children from the audience*)
LITTLE ORCHESTRA: *led by* CHIEF DRUMMER
with FIRST RECORDERS
SECOND RECORDERS
THIRD RECORDERS
ASSISTANT TIMPANIST

THE TALE OF THE FOUR WINDS

There are four WINDS, *two Male (north and south) and two Female (east and west). They control one side each of the arena, where the front rows sit with the appropriate sound effects (triangles, bottles, etc). Each Wind has a signal controlling his row of wind-spirits. Then there are the members of the Court:* the EMPEROR, SHANTI-LO, NANTING-HI, CHIEF JUSTICE, JESTER, EXECUTIONER, SERVANT *and the* EMPRESS – *all of whom are pretty objectionable.*

The OLD HERMIT OF THE HILLS *is good but aged; the* KITCHEN-BOY *is the hero of the story though he does not speak. Opposite him is the* PRINCESS OF THE MOUNTAIN PEOPLE, *beautiful and good; she has two* LADIES *who lead her Retinue of beautiful damsels.*

In addition there is the little ORCHESTRA. *This group is led by the chief* DRUMMER *and consists of recorder-players and timpanists on odd instruments; their music will have been rehearsed.*

Enter FOUR WINDS, *advance to centre, bow to audience.*

NORTH: Greetings, honourable audience, greetings from the northern plains of our esteemed land. I am the North Wind. I bring you the keen, cutting edge of my sweeping wind to freshen your distinguished minds and quicken your admirable spirits. I rule a vast expanse, honourable audience, and I reign supreme. I have great power, and my northern Spirits obey my commands. With one flick of my wrist – *so* – I conjure up my minions moaning at my tail. Do not think I am oppressive if my cold, piercing fingers play upon your skins. I bring ice and snow, thick-ribbed glaciers and glinting icicles. I howl around your ears and penetrate your huddled bodies – but do not think I am unpleasant. I am the North Wind, honourable audience, eldest of my family. (*Lowers hand.*)

SOUTH: And I, honourable audience, am second heir to our esteemed ancestor. I bring you greetings from the abundant forests of the south. I am the South Wind. Forgive my brother if he speaks proudly. He is apt to forget my burning breath, melting the icicles and the snow. I singe and scorch, broil and blaze, smoulder and seethe – all very honourable alliteration to serve this distinguished literary audience. I too have my subject spirits ready to obey my briefest behest. I have but to raise my arm – *thus* – and the hot blasts of fiery furnace sound in your burning ears. We rule the world, my brother and I, from the cold to the clammy, from the frost to the frizzle, the glacier to the grill. True, we have sisters, but they are of little account. I ask your pardon, honourable audience, for detaining your prodigious minds from embracing our unworthy sisters. Do not, I beg you, heed them for long. (*Lowers arm.*)

EAST: Greetings, beautiful and wonderful audience, from the gentle hills of the east. I am the East Wind. I bring you fresh, bracing breezes to lighten your days. Unworthy as I am, I too have spirit friends to help me in my travels over the world. I raise my hand –*thus*– and the spirits of the east play happily on your senses. I bring you rustling, playful caresses. I do not expect your admiration and respect, such as you give my noble brothers, but I hope you will not forget. (*Lowers arm.*)

WEST: And I crave your indulgence, honourable audience, for the West Wind, my unworthy self, bringing greetings from the watery lands, borne of the soft moist tender zephyrs, whose sweet sounds even now can be heard as I hold my hands – *so* – loving joyful spirits tumbling through the clouds and falling softly to the ground, melodious and harmonious music. (*Lowers arm.*)

ALL: Greetings. (*They bow and raise arms to signal;* SPIRITS *play in unison; end.*)

NORTH: Honourable audience, we have a story to unfold – a story to chill you with excitement, a story about a splendid Emperor who ruled his land in gorgeous grandeur.

SOUTH: A story unearthed by the miserable players whom you see beyond us, delved from the depths of the earth – a story about a foolish Kitchen-boy who meddled where he shouldn't.

EAST: A story with a beautiful ending, I hope our honourable audience will find.

WEST: A story that should end in love and happiness, if my sister and I may blow untrammelled.

NORTH/SOUTH: Forgive our forward sisters, sensible and charming audience, they like to dream. . . . the story will unfold as we, my brother and I, will show. (*They raise arms:* SPIRITS *respond.* EAST *and* WEST *raise arms and their* SPIRITS *respond.*)

NORTH: Let us start at the beginning. Some years ago, long before the most honourable ancient of this noble audience first felt my cold commanding power, there was an Emperor, Master of all he surveyed.

SOUTH: He ruled mightily, with a burning power and a chilling command, a great man worshipped by his unworthy subjects.

The four WINDS *begin to move out as the* EMPEROR *and his Court assemble. There is a long roll of the drum as the* EMPEROR *struts round the arena before sitting.*

EMPEROR: Thundering devils with firecrackers on their tails, what's all this? Why am I disturbed from my beauty sleep to assemble my court today? What's all this rabble? Are these all my subjects? Astounding! Look at them, white-faced, grinning like Yucatan yahoos, silly clothes, etc . . . no wonder I'm short of money with a country like this. I'll have to raise more money. Go away! Shoo! Be off with you . . . or stay and keep quiet or I'll string you upside down and tickle you with a peacock feather till you wriggle yourself into a granny knot. (*He sits.*)

Shanti-lo! Nanting-hi! Make haste with that list. This delay is scandalous. Am I to wait for my commands to be executed? Executed! Ha, indeed! How is the cutting edge of your ceremonial weapon, Executioner? It is time we exercised your skill again. It took three blows last time – you are getting too old for your trade, I think.

EXECUTIONER: It was the village tanner, your excellency, he had a leathery skin.

EMPEROR: Do not bandy words with me, you unworthy offspring of a drunken spider. On your scruffy knees and stay below my precious eyesight. (EXECUTIONER *goes down and has to bob up and down to obey him.*)

How dare you interrupt my noble thoughts. Let me see, where was I? Ah yes, the list of citizens with money. The list, where's the list?

SHANTI-LO: Here, great Emperor, held by my unworthy hands for the delectation of your all-consuming eyes. (EMPEROR *takes list and scans it up and down, grunts, sniffs, counts and then holds up his hand.*)

EMPEROR: My pen? Where is my pen, you imbecilic, impotent –?

NANTING-HI: Almighty Emperor, it is ready at your service. I have the ink.

EMPEROR: Where? I see no pen, Prime Minister.

JESTER (*sniggers*): No pen, Emperor? What penalty for hiding the pen, my master?

EMPEROR: Slow torture, you impudent monkey.

JESTER: Then rack yourself, my Emperor, pull out your fingernails! He-he! You are sitting on it.

EMPEROR: Raise me. (*They do so and discover the pen.*) And take out that horrible Jester and bastinado him till he learns to remove pens before I sit down.

(EXECUTIONER *seizes Jester and marches him off, protesting.*)

EMPEROR: The list! Hmmm. I need more money. Tax all the villages by the river; they had a good rice crop last month. No, better than that! Plenipotentiary Extraordinary, fetch me my horoscope. I have a strange feeling that it's my birthday next week.

NANTING-HI: But you have had two this year already – er – Your Excellency.

EMPEROR: I need another birthday party – all my guests can bring money this time. Last time it was precious stones, and some of them were glass. Money this time! I shall have my real birthday next Tuesday. Send out my invitation cards – all to come to my party on pain of confiscation of all property.

SHANTI-LO: Excellency, may my unworthy self interpose a humble suggestion. The genius of your scheme to raise funds cannot be disputed, and our contemptible country rejoices in the brilliance of your worshipful majesty, but . . .

NANTING-HI: There are despicable minds at work, honourable lord, there is talk of obstinate denials of tribute. The people are whispering, my lord, of the omens and the words of the Old Hermit of the Hills. He has been telling dreadful tales. He has been prophesying the end of your glorious rule, he has spoken of the absurd story about the lost son and how he will come back when the East and West Winds

blow together, the lost son of the old unworthy Emperor
whom your revered self had executed as a despicable, vile
and totally inadequate tyrant, since when we have all been
blessed by your own happy rule.

EMPEROR: The Old Hermit of the Hills? I gave orders he was
to be executed. I commanded that no one should mention
the lost son on pain of death. Minister of Justice, have you
not crushed all rumours?

JUSTICE: We have, all-powerful Excellency; no man, woman
or child dares speak of the lost s . . . the ridiculous rumour.
And the Old Hermit is arrested, awaiting your final orders.

EMPEROR: Off with his head immediately. No, send for
him first; I will tell him he lies, that he is a fool and will
die.

SHANTI-LO: The people say the lost son will claim his own
before the next moon. They fly kites to placate the Wind
gods and offer sacrifices to the East and West Winds. They
say the lost son is gathering a huge army over the mountains. They say he has hidden in the kingdom for many
moons but has escaped and will come again. The Old
Hermit says . . .

EMPEROR: Cease this gibberish, you unspeakable pigs, fit only
to eat acorns. The Old Hermit says! Nonsense, all of it. Do
you think I do not know these absurdities? The East and
West Winds blowing together. Pah! Fools, do you think I
have not guarded against this?

JUSTICE (*who has detailed an Attendant to fetch Old Hermit*):
Indeed, O honourable master, you have. Our spies report
no army over the mountain. There are only orange groves
there, oranges and foolish girls dancing. The frontiers of our
land are guarded night and day. The people are closely
watched. The unworthy servants of your magnificence have
exterminated all suspected persons. No one leaves your kind

and gentle care, Your Excellency, unless it is to visit his ancestors.

SHANTI-LO: No one can escape – or return, honourable sir, undetected. But still the people whisper . . .

EMPEROR: The People! Crush them! Tax them! Let them feel my whip! Tell me of any rebel . . . any who try to escape . . .
Re-enter EXECUTIONER *with chastened Jester.*

EMPEROR: What! A miserable jester! Laugh, you malingering monkey!

JESTER (*cowering*): Ha! Ha! (*He laughs weakly; he can hardly walk.*)

Enter EMPRESS.

EMPRESS: What have you been doing, husband, to my little Yangtse Kiang? I heard shrieking in the palace garden, sounding as if a jackal had got among the peacocks again. When I looked out of the window, what should I see but my poor little Jester with his comical feet in the air and that nasty, smelly Executioner friend of yours beating his toes with a cane.

EMPEROR: I was teaching him a lesson; he was mocking me.

EMPRESS: But that's his job; don't be so sensitive, my dear. Give the little man a penny. (*He does not.*) Never mind, Yangtse, the Emperor was only playing. Now then, my dear, I want to have a boy whipped, as soon as possible.

EMPEROR: Of course, my delectable hunk of perfumed refinement, what ever you say. Have you anyone in mind?

EMPRESS: A scullion boy.

EMPEROR: What, a mere kitchen creature! Come now, the Minister of Justice can handle the riff-raff.

EMPRESS: He has. And he escaped.

JUSTICE: But we caught him again, Your Excellency, out on the road to the mountains.

EMPRESS: He insulted my Siamese cat. He kicked him.

EMPEROR: Flog him. Now. Bring him here. And bring us wine.

JUSTICE (*to Executioner*): Bring him.

SHANTI-LO: Your Excellency, while you enjoy the relaxation of wine and flogging, will you honour me with your approval for this little plan of mine to appoint my brother's son to be Minister of Education and my wife's great-aunt as Tax Collector for the southern region.

NANTING-HI: One moment, Your Excellency, I am sure you appreciate the industrious diligence of my own brother's second cousin in running the schools and the tax offices in the south. With all respect to my esteemed friend opposite, I cannot

etc. . . . (*As he speaks the* KITCHEN-BOY *is led in, bound and dishevelled; he is thrown to the ground.*)

EMPRESS: Here is that wretched boy.

EMPEROR: Ah, the pan-scraper, the grease-swiller who kicks royal cats. Why did you kick the Empress's cat? Don't answer that question. You are not fit to wipe the whiskers of our Siamese prize-cat. You shall be flogged before me as I drink my wine, and then be flung out as offal for the carrion crows. Executioner! Proceed.

SHANTI-LO: Your gracious majesty, you know how much I love dear dear Puffy-fluffy. My brother's son's mother sends twenty fat field-mice from the country for . . .

NANTING-HI: . . . your breakfast, dear colleague? I hardly think a royal cat will feed off country mice. My brother's second cousin brings creamed, minced chicken every day for the sweet precious little pettikins.

Meanwhile the EXECUTIONER *has made great play preparing to administer the punishment of the Kitchen-boy. As he raises his arm for the first blow, the* HERMIT OF THE HILLS *is brought in, chained and very old.*

JUSTICE: The Old Hermit of the Hills, Your Excellency.

EMPEROR: Ha! So this is the Old Hermit. Old fool! You shall be executed at once. You mislead my people. You teach them to defy me, you tell them lies and falsehoods with your deceitful prophecies.

OLD HERMIT: Hear me, Emperor. I tell no lies. I tell thee thy days are numbered. Before the rising of the next new moon, thy reign will be completed, thy fate accomplished. Look to the East and West, list to the sighing winds, seek for the rising sun; find ye the golden ball holding the lotus flower, sign of the lost son, heir to this unhappy realm, saviour of a wretched people. Woe to the Emperor, tyrant of his people! Woe to the people, bound to the tyrant! Fear and Death linger in the land! A thousand curses on your ancestors, O cruel Emperor!

While the HERMIT *has proceeded, the* JESTER *has idly opened the small bundle of clothes brought in with the Kitchen-boy and has pocketed a few oddments. He finds a curious golden ball on a chain and is casually swinging this to and fro as the Hermit speaks. He realizes the import of the Hermit's words and begins to study the ball. Everyone else is spellbound by the Hermit.*

EMPEROR (*breaking the spell*): Brainstorming beanshoots! Addled pigeon's eggs! Take that man away. He is mad! I never want to see him again. List to the East and West, rising sun and lotus flower in golden ball. Stupid pifflepaffle, pontificating platitudes. Off with his head! (*He rises to go, then sees the* KITCHEN-BOY *lying on floor.*) And throw that worthless dishcloth over the palace walls; let vultures feed on his filthy flesh. Wife, let that satisfy you.

He departs to roll of drum. Court disperses. Justice leads out the Old Hermit. EXECUTIONER *and* SERVANT *pick up Boy and throw him down. Exeunt. The* JESTER *has now opened the golden ball and revealed a folded lotus flower of paper, which opens up. He looks over the walls at the Boy, thinks hard and then decides to tell the Emperor.*

JESTER (*hobbling out*): Master! Excellency! I know about the lost son! For a golden trinket I will tell you, master. . . . etc

The BOY *lies still, bound hand and foot; the* NORTH WIND *enters.*

NORTH: A foolish boy, honourable audience, he lies stripped and bound, his body exposed to my merciless icy fingers. He dared to defy the Emperor's command, and his punishment was inevitable. He lies still and freezes under my cold, numbing touch; his blood turns to ice. (*He signals to his spirits. The* SOUTH WIND *joins him.*)

SOUTH: The wind changes, and my burning scorching blasts singe his tortured body. He lies still, victim of a power as mighty as my touch. In this heat, all lies still. Imagine, honourable audience, the failing heart in that frail frame, the body warmed by my heat but cold within. And the vultures approach, winging down to pick out his eyes and gorge the flesh from his bones. (*He also has signalled.*)

Music. TWO VULTURES *dance round the body and prepare for the feast. Then the* EAST WIND *enters and scares them away.*

EAST: I bring soft, fragrant breezes to ripple over his body, to send life coursing through his veins. O honourable audience, breathe on him and blow away his tiredness. (*She signals.*)

WEST (*entering*): Arise, Kitchen-boy, and fly! See, with my fragrant breath I loose your bonds. (BOY *stirs, wriggles out of his bonds and obeys the Winds.*) The Emperor learns who you are; even now he rises to strike you down. Rest on our gentle arms and we will fly, fly, fly . . . .

The BOY *dreamlike departs with two Winds. Enter the Emperor and his entourage.*

EMPEROR: So! (*He holds the Jester squirming.*) You found this paper lotus flower in the Kitchen-boy's golden casket. What did the Old Hermit say? 'Seek for the rising sun.' We have sheltered that lost boy here – and you delay telling me?

JESTER: O celestial Emperor, I did not realize, I did not know.

EMPRESS: That vile boy! He struck my dear little Puffy-fluffy. The brute. And all the time he was plotting to kill me.

NANTING-HI: Oh, the risks we have all run. Murdered in our own beds.

SHANTI-LO: Poisoned as we sat eating the food he had touched.

JUSTICE: If only I had known, I would have roasted him alive, torn him limb from limb. The lost son.

EMPEROR: Nonsense! He is an impostor. A mere slave! This is some trick played by that old fool of the hills. Fetch the boy. He must be executed at once.

SHANTI-LO (*after looking over the 'walls'*): Your Excellency, he has gone!

NANTING-HI (*ditto*): Gone!

EMPEROR: Gone? Impossible! He must be found!

EMPRESS: Find him, husband! I cannot bear to think of him alive. After him yourself.

EMPEROR: We will find him. You die (*to Jester*) a lingering death if he escapes. Bring horses! Prime Minister, you will come too. Minister of Justice, raise the alarm. Warn all the outposts on the road to the mountains.

Hobby horses are brought for Emperor, Nanting Hi and Shanti-Lo. They mount.

EMPEROR: Away! And five thousand crowns for the man who brings me his head.

They gallop round and out amid cries, and Music. Enter the BOY, *following the instructions of the Winds.*

SOUTH: And so he runs (*he signals*) staggering through the forests, jumping streams, falling down hillsides and rising

F

once again. (*The* BOY *is miming the actions as he runs round.*)
He does not stop for food but journeys on, his steps slowing
as time goes by; he looks up at the mountain ridge that
towers over the Emperor's land. And he begins to climb.
My burning heat bears him down, crushing him to the hot
soil.

NORTH: But he climbs upwards, onwards, his legs ache, his
heart thumps, he staggers, dizzy, holds his head and feels the
rocks like blocks of ice cut his feet, and his blood leaves a
trail in the snow like crimson peonies on apple blossom. He
comes to a roaring mountain torrent. At last he is halted; he
can go no farther. (NORTH WIND *throws down and unfurls
cloth river.*)

EAST (*entering with rope*): But he finds a long tendril and
throws it across the foaming waters. (BOY *does so and the*
WEST *and* EAST *hold it aloft;* BOY *crosses river.*) And deli-
cately, like a spider on a thread, he eases himself over.

NORTH (*frowning and making a mimed barrier*): But what does
he find barring his way? A solid rock face, impenetrable,
only a few icy nooks and crannies to help him across.

SOUTH: And a hot blast of air from my fiery southern furnace
blow in his face.

WEST: He goes on, treading gingerly the rocky ledges, fingers
clinging to icy crevices, edging his way slowly along and
across, while my soft wind urges him on.

WEST: And, with one gentle push of wind behind him, he
reaches the top and runs over the last bitter barrier, down,
down into a new world of gentle trees and singing birds. In
a clearing he stops by a crystal-clear stream, falls to bathe his
parched lips and lies there motionless.

Music. The MOUNTAIN PEOPLE *enter, singing and dancing.
The* PRINCESS *goes round, smiling at audience; her two*
LADIES *lead two trains of dancing girls. The Boy is not noticed.*

PRINCESS: We will rest here, where the silver birch and the willow shade us from the sun.

LADY 1: Princess of the Mountain People, listen to the song of the mountains.

LADY 2 (*sings*): Let the wild swans northward fly
Born on warm south winds;
Shoot not the wild swans from the south
Or, if you will, shoot the winged pain
That they may ne'er be parted.

LADY 1: Sweet music to fit this peaceful bower. Saadia, run to the stream and fetch the Princess water to drink.

LADY 2 runs over to stream and sees Boy. She screams. All run over to see him.

LADY 2: Madam, oh princess, there is a boy here, a young man. I think he is dead.

LADY 1: He is not dead. Do you see, his eyes stir and open (GIRLS *provide refrain of 'Yes' to these remarks now.*)

LADY 2: Is he not handsome?

LADY 1: Is he a prince?

LADY 2: Look at his hands! He is no prince. He is a peasant.

LADY 1: Yet he looks noble. Let us attend him. Quickly, water for his brow.

LADY 2: Look at his wounds. Poor man!

LADY 1: He has escaped from the Emperor. Who is he?

Sound of galloping drums, etc., as EMPEROR and his henchmen arrive.

EMPEROR: Ha! At last! We succeed. (*He dismounts.*) Princess, for such I take you to be, I crave your indulgence.

LADY 1: Princess indeed, Emperor from over the mountain, daughter of the ruler of this land.

EMPEROR: Pray convey my respects to your dear father with humble and unworthy apologies for this intrusion on his esteemed privacy. I come to claim a small article which has been unaccountably lost.

LADY 2: And what small article brings the great Emperor to our peaceful land?

EMPEROR: That boy! That filthy wretch standing there. My Kitchen-boy!

LADY 1: Kitchen-boy! You pursue a Kitchen-boy?

EMPEROR: Yes. Well, no, he's the lost – ah, yes, a Kitchen-boy.

PRINCESS (*to Boy*): Is this true? (BOY *nods; she looks sad.*)

LADY 2: The Princess may not save a servant. Will you not spare him?

EMPEROR: Spare him! I waste no time. He will die now. Nanting-hi, give me your sword, I shall strike this miserable recreant myself. You are no lost son, no saviour of the people, and I soil my hands spilling your blood. But I shall crush this Hermit's lies with your death.

> The EMPEROR *advances with sword. The* BOY *held by Shanti-lo kneels. As he raises sword, a Gong sounds and all freeze. Enter* WINDS.

NORTH: And so the poor boy dies, honourable audience, as my moaning minions sweep down from over the mountains. (*Signals.*)

SOUTH: He was a brave little fellow, of course. What he has suffered! And how magnificently he fought against my brother and me! But now he is caught, exhausted, poor Kitchen-boy, and he must meet this final death's blow like a man. (*Signals.*)

WEST: Oh honourable audience, shall he perish so sadly? Does he not deserve a happier fate? Listen while I summon my western spirits to blow against my brothers.

EAST: And I too will plead for your sympathy, O gentle and kind-hearted audience. You would not see him die? Listen while I hold hands with my sister to defeat the harsh rule of my brothers, North and South. (*They both signal and there ensues a battle of noises from the attendant spirits to see who wins. Gradually the* EAST *and* WEST *vanquish the* NORTH *and the* SOUTH, *who slink out.*)

EAST: Now, brave boy, rise up and fight.

Gong sounds and characters unfreeze.

EMPEROR: Ha! You die, insufferable dog! (*As he raises sword high, the* WEST WIND *signals, and the* EMPEROR *staggers as if blown off balance by wind. The* BOY *throws off Shanti-lo, takes his sword and advances.* EAST WIND *signals, great noise as* BOY *thrusts sword through Emperor's clothes.* SHANTI-LO *and* NANTING-HI *fall on knees. The* GIRLS *leap for joy and dance round Boy.* PRINCESS *stands smiling, and the* BOY *is brought to her. As he kneels, she raises him. Gong sounds. All freeze.*)

NORTH (*advancing*): But this is preposterous. This Boy cannot be allowed to take the hand of a Princess, true daughter of a ruler.

SOUTH: Honourable audience, send him back to the kitchens where he belongs. The Hermit's prophecies have been fulfilled; this Boy happened to carry a golden ball with a paper lotus flower within it. Coincidence! He belongs to the kitchen.

NORTH: Send him home to the kitchen, and to his poor simple mother, who awaits him in her crumbling cottage.

WEST: Oh lovely and beautifully-minded audience, do not send him back to the kitchens. Does he not look fine beside the Princess?

EAST: Let him stay by her side, even if he is of lowly birth. He can protect her.

SOUTH: A foolish thought. She has her father's guards. No, follow my advice. Send him packing. Shout 'Kitchen' for me and my brother!

EAST: Shout 'Princess' for me and my sister!

The audience, it is to be hoped, raises the roof.

Either North/South or East/West win. Whichever side loses has this final speech.

WIND: Honourable audience, our tale is at an end. You have decided the fate of this Boy. Do not judge us too harshly, for we meant all for the best. All cannot be accomplished for, though the wind blows where it listeth, there are alas four winds.

Bow to winning winds and exeunt.

Music and procession out, with PRINCESS *taking Boy's hand or not taking Boy's hand. Two* WINDS *depart, bowing to prone Emperor.*

Then to the audience.

END

Under Beachy Head

Portrait of a Sussex Seaside Resort

BY MICHAEL MORLEY

CHARACTERS

THE NARRATOR
MRS PUFFIN
MR PUFFIN
MR TUBB
MRS TUBB
TWO TUBB BOYS
MR AND MRS HONEY
MR PONSONBY
MRS PONSONBY
MR WARBLEDON
EMILY BROWN
MR AND MRS THYME
CAPTAIN COD
REV JOSIAH PONTIFF
P. C. PERIWINKLE
BENNY GILL
NED PUNCHBOWL
WAITER

UNDER BEACHY HEAD

*Before the house lights dim, the arena-stage is 'laid' with five folding
tables and chairs prone, with tablecloths near them, small trays
with breakfast crockery and cutlery, and other dark blankets
or bedcovers arranged on stage. When lights go out, the cast
enters and lies as in beds under cloths, and each sits up to deliver
lines. Spotlights will of course be helpful.*

When the play starts, the audience is aware of the NARRATOR,
*perhaps spotlit centre, and figures lying all round; but there is
little light at first.*

Thus: darkness turning to a very dim light as the NARRATOR
*moves into the arena. A clock chimes comfortingly; an owl hoots
and a faint wind sighs.*

NARRATOR: A scurrying wind creeps along the crest of the
Downs, and then scuttles sideways down the hill, to vanish
in the sleeping jaws of the town. The houses turn in their
sleep, breathing the gull-free air. On the beach, the sea
murmurs, chuckling drowsily over its shingle pillow; it
pulls the caressing black blanket of silence closer about its
shoulders. The lulling of its swaying movements rocks the
town in hushabye sleep, and away to the right the pale nightwatchman, Beachy Head, puckers its brow and peers
watchfully at nothing, out at sea. Nothing peers watchfully
back. The lighthouse, the nightwatchman's lantern, lolls
drunkenly at his pale feet, throwing white beams of light
out to sea, where they drown, and all the trees around the
town softly whisper the scandal to one another.

Then, like an unexpected guest, a hushed dawn scrambles

nimbly over the outlying rooftops of the dreamy town and spreads wide its open arms. It pushes the night rudely out of the way and strides briskly down between the house fronts, where curtain-clad eyelids resist the invading hordes of day. Dawn shouts its challenge aloud, but in reality it is as quiet as the dewfall.

The town capitulates with hardly a murmur, and in the misty distance the early morning victory bells of milk crates chime, like Himalayan prayer-wheels. The chink and clink of bottles – whiter than white – ring round the streets and disturb the slumbers of dreaming residents and visitors. They stir uneasily, and their dreams merge mistily in the morning air. They dream of

– cue for entry of BENNY GILL, *the milkman. During the next sequence he moves from place to place, keeping to the edge of the arena. The sleepers lie still while the voices dream:*

VOICES DREAMING: Channel swimming
fish and chips
love and bosoms
any more for the lighthouse
sorry, no vacancies
another one for the road
no hawkers
Lady Penelope
wipe your feet
the rent
no baths before ten
the rates
the rent
the rates
the rent
death
life

NARRATOR: the milkman whistles his way down the street, milk crate swinging. He arrives at

MRS PUFFIN (*as if talking in her sleep, in a voice of obviously assumed refinement*): Seaview, Private Hotel, bed and breakfast or full board, very reasonable terms, h and c in all rooms, all mod cons and W.C.s that flush first time.

NARRATOR: and leaves the morning milk as the owl hoots like a lightship in the trees. Inside Seaview, Mrs Puffin stirs and sits up with a jerk as the alarm clock jangles.

MRS PUFFIN (*half asleep, impatiently, in her natural voice*): All right, all right, shut up, shut up. What's the time? Half-past six. Another day. Another day of slavery for these stupid holiday-makers. Hope you have a nice day! ugh! where's my mask? Hey!

NARRATOR: and she picks up her stick and thumps on the partition to wake her husband, puffing asthmatic Mr Puffin, who is shoved away in a cupboard for the night because there is no room in a bed for him at the inn. He dreams

MR PUFFIN (*half asleep*): I dream of a golden palace, all marble and harem, with a bed ten feet wide, room for me and half a dozen . . . (*Mrs Puffin's stick thumps*) . . . for Mr and Mrs Puffin of 'Sea-view'. Yes, dear, time to get up to prepare for our beloved guests! A cup of tea for those who pay . . .

MR TUBB (*dreaming*): Pay, pay, pay packets on Friday.

NARRATOR: Mr Tubb, on holiday from a Midlands motor manufacturing mausoleum, where he manipulates the main chassis screws with machine-like precision, fumbles in his dreams over his wages, which his wife has counted out each weekend for the family holiday in the Suntrap of the South.

MRS TUBB: 46 pounds, 47 pounds, 48 pounds, 49 pounds, 50 pounds . . .

NARRATOR: ... while her two precious perishers fight in their dreams.

TWO TUBB BOYS: You did. I didn't. You did. I didn't ... etc.

NARRATOR: In the next room the honeymoon couple snuggle closer as the morning breeze intrudes on their warm, true-heart, hot-bottle privacy.

MR HONEY: Aaah! Mmmmm! Darling? Darling?

MRS HONEY: Yes, darling?

MR HONEY: Nothing. Just, darling ...

NARRATOR: and in the best front room with verandahed windows and potted geraniums, Mr and Mrs Posonby slumber under their over-stuffed eiderdown bed dreaming of

MRS PONSONBY (*dreaming*): my boy, my son, in his bright new navy blue suit.

MR PONSONBY (*dreaming*): Sub-Lieutenant Richard Ponsonby, late of Dartmouth.

NARRATOR: Steaming home to mother's arms from sunny Zanzibar.

MRS PONSONBY: Dicky, Dicky, come to me
Over the rolling, briny sea.

MR PONSONBY: Fine figure of a boy, credit to his father.

MRS PONSONBY: Here he comes from east of Aden, proud and gallant sailor.

MR PONSONBY: Don't rock the boat, Alice, I'm listening to the news.

MRS PONSONBY: Here he comes, all shipshape and Bristol-fashioned.

MR PONSONBY: Gilt-edged securities are up $\frac{1}{8}$ or $\frac{1}{4}$ for medium- and longer-dated issues.

MRS PONSONBY: Through the Bay of Biscay, full speed ahead, Richard Ponsonby at the helm, second-in-command.

MR PONSONBY: Platinums pursue a downward course with Union 6½ p lower at 113½ p.

MRS PONSONBY: Sinking, the ship's sinking! He's being pulled down into the sea, the cruel green sea.

MR PONSONBY: Lloyds hardening by a quarter per cent. Shipping a particularly weak section.

MRS PONSONBY: I see waves washing over his head – he's drowning!

MR PONSONBY: All right; sell out. Abandon shipping . . .

MRS PONSONBY: Richard! Richard!

NARRATOR: and they clutch each other in the darkness of their dreams rocked on the waves of their private fears.

(During this sequence, sounds of waves or ships have occurred; at the end the PONSONBYS *cling to each other and then gradually subside as the spotlight fades from them.)*

In a single room, number 25, with a view of the sea if you stand on the wash-basin, Mr Warbledon, the London schoolmaster with mathematical master-mind, puts a tick and a loving cross beside the vital statistics of his dream . . .

MR WARBLEDON *(dreaming)*: 15 – 20 – 38; 20 – 15 – 48; 38 – 26 – 38 . . . Ah!

EMILY BROWN *(dreaming)*: Take your filthy mind off me!

NARRATOR: Emily Brown, shop assistant in Leeds, turns over the fashion-page of her glossy magazine mind and dreams of . . .

EMILY: wearing a silk sash with Beauty Queen of Sussex 1970.

NARRATOR: . . . written across her undulating front.

MR WARBLEDON: Oh, Miss Brown, I wish you were mine.

EMILY *(sleepily)*: I wish I was being crowned by Dirk Bogarde.

MR WARBLEDON: Oh, Miss Brown, I wish you were . . .

EMILY: I wish I was being crowned by Dirk . . .

They repeat, dropping a word each time, until

MR WARBLEDON: Oh . . .

EMILY: I . . .

NARRATOR: I-slands of lonely make-believe, they lie lonely in the sea of their dreams. (*He turns to regard Mr Puffin.*) Asthmatic Mr Puffin, hacking to himself, shuffles into the kitchen to make the morning tea for the guests.

MR PUFFIN (*dressing-gowned, on way out*): Here's your morning cup of sea-brine, madam.

NARRATOR (*moving across*): In a box-like bungalow across the way, the Milkman leaves one pint, half a pint for Tabby, Tubby and Tibby, half for Mr and Mrs Thyme tick-tocking away their dreams to the beat of the old grandfather clock in the corner.

MR AND MRS THYME (*popping up together*):
Darby and Joan, we live together
Snug in bed like birds of a feather
We make the beds and wash and dry
Enjoying retirement until we die
And everything you like to mention
Is bought out of our old-age pension.
They subside.

NARRATOR: The Milkman heaves to by Compass Cottage and without so much as an 'Ahoy' drops his bottle for Captain Cod asleep in his pitching and rolling hammocking bed, with a hot water bottle of rum by his side.

CAPTAIN COD: Milkman! Two pints! One bitter and one mild.

NARRATOR: And he settles to dream of

CAPTAIN COD: haulin' in the nets off Beachy Head filled with shoals of glitterin', shinin', gleamin' fifty-pence pieces and keel-haulin' the lighthouse-lovin' landlubbers who swamp my boat. Any more for the keelhaul?

NARRATOR: Mentally removing his shoes and hat as he tip-toes up the aisle of the vicarage path, the Milkman offers a pint to be consecrated by the Reverend Josiah Pontiff, who raises his hand to bless and then has a nightmare about his congregation.

THE REV. J. PONTIFF (*sitting up with a jerk*): Curse you all! *The* MILKMAN *hastily retreats and moves towards* P.C. PERIWINKLE *who strolls in.*

NARRATOR: And P. C. Periwinkle homeward plods his weary way.

P.C. PERIWINKLE: 'Mornin' all.

NARRATOR: And he thinks of . . .

P.C. PERIWINKLE: retiring to a nice little semi-detached in Polegate, away from rowdy holiday makers, the traffic and the beat.

He meets the Milkman – light improving.

MILKMAN: Mornin', Sarge.

P.C. PERIWINKLE: Mornin', Benny.

MILKMAN: Well, how's the arm of the law this fine morning? Caught any bank robbers with that little finger of yours?

P.C. PERIWINKLE: Not exactly; it's my feet that are killing me.

MILKMAN: What you want is to soak them each night in yoghurt, natural unflavoured yoghurt. (*He holds one up.*)

P.C. PERIWINKLE (*heavily*): I'm sure you're right, Benny; send me round a dozen and charge them to the station. Well, I must be on my way.

MILKMAN: That's right. Me too. Time's getting on.

As they depart, MRS PUFFIN, *from the centre of the arena where she has been lying, sounds the gong loudly and persistently. This is the signal for all to rise – only those at Seaview staying on stage. They erect tables with cloths, place trays for breakfast and settle scene. Offstage the radio is offering a Jimmy Young-type record programme.*

MR TUBB (*doing exercises*): Stop mucking about, you kids, and settle down to your breakfast. 'Morning. (*To Mr Ponsonby, who has just collected his* Financial Times *and who makes no reply.*)

MRS TUBB: Gary, sit still. I'm ashamed of you, really I am. Good morning! (*To Emily Brown.*)

EMILY BROWN: Good morning! (*She smiles and then freezes as* MR WARBLEDON *hopefully replies.*)

MR WARBLEDON: Good morning! (*He retreats into his breakfast.*)

   Enter MR PUFFIN *with trolley of cereals and* MRS PUFFIN *with teapots for tables.*

MRS PUFFIN: Good morning. A nice cup of tea to start the day!

MR TUBB (*to the Honeys*): Hello, there. Sleep well, then?

   The HONEYS *react in confusion and simper.*

MR PUFFIN: 'Morning, Mrs Tubb. I trust you had a good night.

MRS TUBB: Oh yes, thanks, Mr Puffin. Very well, thank you. Lovely beds; I can tell the difference from last year.

MRS PUFFIN: Yes, we've got new mattresses, y' know, interior sprung. Got them on every bed now. Oh yes, so important to sleep well when you're on holiday. We try to look after our guests. (*She moves over to Mr and Mrs Ponsonby, and as she speaks a double dialogue starts . . .*)

MRS PUFFIN: 'Morning, Mr and Mrs Ponsonby. Lovely day for the holiday.

MRS PONSONBY: Good morning, yes, it is quite promising. I was only saying to my husband how nice it will be if the sun is shining while our son is with us, wasn't I, dear?

MR TUBB: Look, you two, eat up them cornflakes. We're not wasting any food while we're here so have a good breakfast.

MRS TUBB: and keep your feet still, Alan. Stop kicking the chair.

MR TUBB: and shurrup while I'm reading.

MR PONSONBY (*disturbed from his paper*): Eh? Son shining? Sun? Oh Richard, yes, should be here today.

MRS PONSONBY: He's in the Navy, you know, been away on a long cruise.

MRS PUFFIN: Oh yes, he'll be very comfy in the back single room, nicely aired.

MRS PONSONBY: I wonder if he'll be used to a hammock, dear boy. Do you think he needs a hammock, dear?

MR PONSONBY: Eh? what, a hammock? What the devil do you want a hammock for?

ALAN TUBB: Did Lancashire win, Dad?

GARY TUBB: 'Course they didn't, stupid.

ALAN: I bet they did ⎫
GARY: They didn't ⎭ etc.

MR TUBB: Shurrup, you two. I'll tell you who won. No one; 'Match abandoned without a ball being bowled.'

MRS TUBB: Now get on with your breakfast.

MRS PUFFIN *has moved away and departs.* MR TUBB *leans over . . .*

MR TUBB (*sociable-like*): Well, Mr Ponsonby, it's a lovely day. Raining cats and dogs in the north. Just right for the beach, eh? Promised to take the children down as soon as possible. I don't suppose you've got children to worry about now . . .

MR PONSONBY (*un-cooperative*): Children? Well, no – humph . . . bit past that.

MRS PONSONBY: But we do have our son joining us today. He's an officer in the Royal Navy; due on leave today. He's coming here to join us. He's a wonderful boy . . . you'll adore him.

MR TUBB: Yes, I'm sure. Very nice. (*Out of his depth.*) *Silence. Sound of eating. Papers.* MR *and* MRS HONEY *bill*

G

and coo. EMILY BROWN *starts to make up.* MR WARBLEDON *spies at her over his paper.*

NARRATOR: The morning rites continue: breakfast in Seaview, and a sea of silence flows over the sands of their small-talk. They eat and drink and hide their secret thoughts.

MR WARBLEDON: I shall propose to her when I have met her properly. How to introduce myself . . . will she drop something . . . or shall I accidentally bump into her table . . . or shall I walk up to her and say bravely and boldly, 'Miss Brown, I want you' . . .

MR PONSONBY: Seaview isn't what it used to be. Tone of the place going down; same with the town. Too popular these days; it's all these northerners. Uncouth lot! Well, look at that family, noisy, vulgar, no manners. We should have gone to a hotel.

MRS PUFFIN: Spring interior mattresses! I hope she don't go snooping round her kids' beds. Hurry up, you miseries, finish your food and get off my premises.

EMILY BROWN: It must be lovely staying at the Grand.

MRS PONSONBY: I do hope Richard will like a seaside holiday.

MR and MRS HONEY: Darling! Darling! Darling! Darling!

MR TUBB: Stuck-up lot here this year. We'll go to Morecambe next year.

MR PUFFIN: Get the washing-up done, then down to the Red Lion for a quick snifter.

ALAN TUBB: Why can't we go to Pontin's?

GARY TUBB: Butlin's!

MRS TUBB: Nice to see the family so contented.

MRS PUFFIN (*breaking the sequence, advancing to centre*): Well, it's lovely and sunny outside, everyone. Lovely day. I should make the most of it and get out quickly, so if you'll leave the breakfast things now and get your things ready for the beach . . . I'll make sandwiches if you like – only five bob a pack . . .

The visitors gossip out as the clock strikes nine. MR PUFFIN *takes out the tables and chairs, helped by some visitors on their way out.* MRS PUFFIN *uses the trolley to collect breakfast things. The* NARRATOR *speaks.*

NARRATOR: The day breaks. And the sea breaks its lazy back on the pebbles of the beach. The sun gathers its strength for the labours of the day. Residents and visitors are wending their way down to the front. (*Enter the* MILKMAN *with portable ice-cream gear.*) Here comes Benny Gill, the morning milkman, cheerily walking to his ice-cream stall – and there is Ned Punchbowl, the deckchair attendant. (*Enter* NED PUNCHBOWL *with deckchairs –* BENNY *and* NED *wave and exchange a greeting.*)

And in a little backroom at the Pier Theatre a pianist practises his Fol-de-Rol bread and butter music . . .

Sound of piano playing 'Good old Sussex by the Sea'. BENNY *and* NED *start a soft-shoe shuffle and are joined by* P.C. PERIWINKLE *and* CAPTAIN COD. NED *sings the words as the four weave in and out; and the visitors arrive to fill the arena, settling down as the four 'dancers' disperse and depart at each corner.*

MR *and* MRS PONSONBY *settle in deckchairs, she with her letters to read, he with the* Financial Times.

The TUBB FAMILY *litters the ground, two deckchairs, the children playing.*

EMILY BROWN *sunbathes on a mat, making play with suntan lotion.*

MR WARBLEDON *sits under a towel and wriggles into a discreet costume.*

THE HONEYS *lie coyly by each other, reading domestic literature.*

The THYMES *are also in deckchairs with rugs; he sleeps, she knits.*

The strains of the piano die away; the sea sounds and sea-gulls cry. The visitors have talked and improvised while settling down, but now the scene is suddenly quiet and motionless.

At the four corners appear CAPTAIN COD, *the* REVD. J. PONTIFF, BENNY GILL *and* MR PUFFIN. NED PUNCH-BOWL *slowly goes round collecting deckchair dues.*

NARRATOR: Now life slows down to a standstill. The sun, like a wealthy Renaissance Prince, showers his gold upon the town, and rich and poor, young and old, resident and visitor, prostrate themselves before the almighty. A fanfare blows down from the bandstand. (*Sound of brassband music faintly.*) Bodies bask in bikinis and sunsuits, minds drift into an easy sunwashed daze, God's in his heaven, all's well with the world. And, from the four corners of the seafront, the summertime traders ply their wares.

NED PUNCHBOWL *exit. Speaking from four corners,*

CAPTAIN COD: Any more for the lighthouse? A lovely day for the briny!

REVD. PONTIFF: All this sun-worship, and yet my church is full on Sunday!

MR PUFFIN: I like to come down of a morning and see the sights.

BENNY GILL: Ice-cream! Icecream! Here I stand with my barrel of ice lollies, cornets, wafers, choc-ices, zooms and top-tens. Can't stand the stuff myself.

CAPTAIN COD: We're off any moment now. *The Sussex Belle* ploughing her way over the waves with a cargo of Londoners, Brummagers, Scousers, Sussex men and women in minis and midis.

REVD. PONTIFF: Perhaps the pagan people are drawn to a higher spirituality by this body-browning business. By the end of the week they grow tired of the flesh and visit the church for spiritual sunbathing.

MR PUFFIN: I walk along the prom looking down on all those lovely limbs sprawled out on the pebbles. Many's the time I've almost fallen over the edge looking at – some old dearie in a deckchair.

BENNY GILL: Ha! here come two more customers. (*The Tubb children approach him.*) Two fivepenny cornets. Certainly, young man. (*Provides them.*)

CAPTAIN COD (*to Mr Ponsonby, who has risen for a stroll*): Now sir, what about a trip round the lighthouse?

MR PONSONBY: Thank you, but not today.

CAPTAIN COD: Ever been on the sea, ma'am?

MRS PONSONBY: No, but my son has. He's in the Royal Navy, arriving at Portsmouth today, just back from the Middle East – he'll be here soon. Perhaps he'll go with you tomorrow.

CAPTAIN COD: Ye-es, perhaps he will, ma'am.

REVD. PONTIFF (*circulating*): Hello, Mr and Mrs Thyme, how are you?

MR and MRS THYME: Hello, Vicar, very well, thank you.

MRS THYME: It's a pity the beach gets so crowded in the summer. I prefer the town at Easter-time, really, before the visitors arrive.

REVD. PONTIFF: We must share our blessings with those less fortunate than ourselves. Well, very nice to see you. Good-bye, God bless. (*He moves out.*)

MR PUFFIN: Hello; there's that funny young fellow who's staying at our place. What's he up to?

MR WARBLEDON (*has risen, now moving circumspectly over*): Oh . . . hello, it's Miss Brown.

EMILY BROWN: Oh, hello. (*Turns away.*)

MR WARBLEDON: I wondered if you could help me with this

clue for the crossword – er – it says 2 across er . . . (*Rebuffed, he sits down.*)

MR PUFFIN: You'll never make it, chum. She's not your kind. Or rather you're not her kind.

BENNY GILL (*who has served the Tubb boys*): There we are, then – coming back for another in a while, I expect. Be seeing you.

　　The TUBB BOYS *return to places licking ices as* MR TUBB *rises.*

MR TUBB: Well, then, what about a quick dip. Let's see how cold it is. (*He gingerly steps over pebbles down to the edge of the arena and dips his toe in.*)

MRS TUBB: Mind that oil-tar, Gary. There now, look, you've put your foot on it. Don't put your foot down there – mind that towel. Look what you've done now! Oh, sit down, put your feet in the air and I'll clean the muck off them. And put that ice-cream down. (GARY, *protesting, sits and places cornet where Mr Tubb has been sitting.*)

MR TUBB (*retreating*): Brrr! Bit cold still, I'll wait a bit longer.
　　(*He sits – on the cornet.*)
　　It's perishing cold out of the water, too.
　　(*He discovers the cause, and, when* GARY *rises indignantly, clips him one.*)
　　Now I'll *have* to have a swim – to clean it off!
　　(*He hobbles off.*)

NARRATOR: The sea approaches nearer. Its tongue licks the pebbles and arms of foaming suds extend to embrace the towels, buckets and spades, deckchairs and lilos. The heat is impressive, oppressive, heavy, ominous . . . Suddenly!
　　(*Crash of thunder; all sit up.*)
　　The Suntrap of the South closes with a snap!
　　(*Rain begins to pelt down.*)
Caught in a mesh of rain, the beach visitors gather their gear

and scamper away, escaping the pitiless pelting of the cloud-burst thunderstorm.

(MR TUBB *enters*, NED PUNCHBOWL *enters – and all start to exeunt severally.*)

The beach is alone.

And the visitors and residents move to their hideaways and await the end of the day. The Honeys run back to Seaview under his macintosh; . . . they share everything. (*The* HONEYS *run across under a raincoat.*) Mr and Mrs Thyme arrive home, with a shake of umbrella and with one flick of the wrist banish the clouds from their skies.

The THYMES *have entered.* MR THYME *takes off his plastic mac and goes out;* MRS THYME *stands shaking her umbrella and tut-tutting to herself.*

MR THYME (*re-entering*): I can't get the picture, my dear.

MRS THYME: Give it time to warm up, dear.

MR THYME: It's a man's best friend, is television. (*Exit.*)

MRS THYME: And a woman's, dear. (*Exit.*)

NARRATOR: The Tubb boys, having lost their sand-castle to the rain, besiege Seaview like swashbuckling buccaneers on the rampage. (*The* TUBB FAMILY *bicker their way across, and, as* MR *and* MRS TUBB *go out,* MRS PUFFIN *snatches the spades from the two duelling boys.*)

MRS PUFFIN: And we'll have them nasty things left outside, if you please. And that bucket, sloppy wet thing.

GARY TUBB: I've got a crab in there. (*Shows it.*)

MRS PUFFIN: Don't you bring that in here!

MR PUFFIN (*taking bucket*): Don't worry, sonny. I'll give it to Mrs Puffin for her supper. (*Exit with boys.*)

MRS PUFFIN: 'Evening, Mr Warbledon, will you be in for supper?

MR WARBLEDON: Oh yes – er no – that is, have you seen – ah, Miss Brown?

MR TUBB (*changing shirt*): Saw her standing in the bus shelter down the road, keeping out of the rain. 'Evening, Mrs Puffin.

MR WARBLEDON: I won't be in for supper, Mrs Puffin. I'll just fetch my umbrella.

MRS TUBB (*changed*): We thought we'd go out after supper, just the two of us, you know; have a bit of Bingo by the sea.

MRS PUFFIN: Well, it's sausages and chips this evening; followed by rice pudding. Ready when you are . . . (*Exeunt.*)

NARRATOR: While Mr and Mrs Ponsonby sit at a table, crisp and sumptuous, in the Golden Dragon Restaurant.

   (*During the previous sequence at Seaview, one dinner-table and two chairs have been placed at other end of arena. A WAITER, with food trolley, etc., is standing by.*)

   Any minute now, they will raise their eyes to the doorway to look for the saltfresh shining face of Richard Ponsonby, R.N., the little pride and joy in his navy blue.

MR PONSONBY (*studying menu*): Smoked salmon or avocado pear; chicken or steak; . . . humph . . (etc.).

MRS PONSONBY (*staring over*): No fish, my dear, not with Richard coming.

MR PONSONBY: We'll have one avocado and one paté de la maison. Then two stocks – er, steaks, done rarely and . . . etc.

WAITER: And your wine, sir?

MR PONSONBY: Let me see the wine list.

MRS PONSONBY (*peering*): Arthur, is that Richard over there? – I can't quite see without my glasses.

MR PONSONBY: What? Where? Richard! (*He rises, then checks as he sees P.C. Periwinkle talking to Waiter.*)

   No, that's not Richard. Nothing like. It's a policeman.

WAITER (*returning*): Excuse me, sir, there's a message for you (*gives card.*)

MR PONSONBY: Good heavens, he wants to see me. Says he has something to tell us, about Sub-Lieutenant Ponsonby. (*He reads.*)

MRS PONSONBY: Richard! Oh, there's been an accident.

MR PONSONBY (*rising*): Stay here, my dear, I'll see him.

MRS PONSONBY: He's drowned. I know he's drowned. My dream this morning. I saw him falling through the waves, clutching at seaweed and bubbles, drowning in the deep ocean!

WAITER: Are you all right, madam?

MRS PONSONBY: My son, Richard, my son! (*P.C. Periwinkle leaves.*)

MR PONSONBY (*returning*): I'm afraid it's bad news, Alice.

MRS PONSONBY: Richard!

MR PONSONBY: He won't be coming here to join us. (*Sitting.*)

MRS PONSONBY: Never, never!

MR PONSONBY: His ship's been diverted to the Irish Sea.

MRS PONSONBY: Richard! (*She is distrait; he looking at menu.*)

MR PONSONBY: They've been sent to help a ship in distress.

MRS PONSONBY: In distress?

MR PONSONBY: Yes, so he won't be docking for a few days.

MRS PONSONBY: He's all right?

MR PONSONBY: Who? Richard? Of course. Thoughtful of him to get a message to us. Very nice police constable.

MRS PONSONBY: Richard is safe! He's not drowned!

MR PONSONBY: Now what shall we have to drink?

MRS PONSONBY (*rising*): Nothing. I don't want anything. Take me away from here. (MR PONSONBY *rises, mystified by his wife's behaviour. They leave; the waiter takes away the dinner-table, etc.*)

NARRATOR: And stunned by memories of her dreams, she leaves, filled with an empty longing no dinner can ever satisfy.

(CAPTAIN COD *steps out and drinks on his way*.)
Captain Cod downs his tenth pint at the Mariner's Arms and steps into the night. He meets P.C. Periwinkle . . .

CAPTAIN COD: Evening, Commodore. Stormy night to-night.

P.C. PERIWINKLE: Stormy for some, Captain Cod. Mind you go straight home.

CAPTAIN COD: Aye, aye, skipper. (*Light dimming fast . . .*)

NARRATOR: And he bumps into Mr Warbledon, a ship that passes in the night thinking of Emily Brown, whom he sees . . .

　　As CAPTAIN COD *goes out, enter* EMILY BROWN *and* BENNY GILL *arm in arm.*

EMILY BROWN: . . . going out with the milkman, and very nice too. Oh, hello, Mr Warbledon (*They go out, leaving Mr Warbledon.*)

MR WARBLEDON: Oh, Miss Brown! (*He departs disconsolately.*)

NARRATOR: And Mrs Tubb puts the children to bed with a fairy story.

MRS TUBB (*to the Tubb boys, dressed for bed and preparing to lie on the floor under blankets they bring in*): and, if you children talk and play about in bed, I'll fetch your father to give you a good smack on your b t m s.

　　A clock chimes; the lights are very low; the arena is occupied by the visitors and residents in night attire, settling down in same positions as for start.

NARRATOR: Night falls gently. The waves roll rippling over the houses, drowning the wakeful thoughts, and, as the owl hoots mournfully, the residents and visitors return to their dream holiday in the Suntrap of the South.

MR and MRS THYME (*sitting up*): We're as snug as a bug, as a pea in a pod,

We've watched our favourite programme till our heads
began to nod.

We don't ask much, but there's one thing we might
mention –

We'd both like a rise in our old age pension.

MR and MRS HONEY: Darling! sweetheart! dearest! love!

MR WARBLEDON: 15 – 20 – 38; 20 – 15 – 48; 38 – 26 – 38 . . .
aah!

EMILY BROWN: I want to be crowned by Dirk, not the milkman. Dirk!

CAPTAIN COD: Heave ho! I've got the sea inside me tonight.
Batten down the hatches, lads, or we'll sink. Heave ho!

MRS PUFFIN: I'm staying at the Hilton, Mayfair; aah . . . with
twenty men to wait on me. I'll sleep till eleven. (*Yawns.*)

MR PUFFIN: Ho, ho, I've got twenty wives to wait on me. I
shan't sleep all night. (*Yawns.*)

MRS PONSONBY: Dicky, Dicky, come to me
Over the rolling briny sea!

MR PONSONBY: Shipping shares are slipping; slipping shares
are shipping.

REVD. PONTIFF: 'Oh, hear us when we cry to thee, for those
in peril on the sea.'

MRS TUBB: The children have grown up . . . oh, what a
relief!

TUBB BOYS: You did, I didn't, you did, I didn't . . .

MR TUBB: I dream of winning the football pools.

VOICES: channel swimming
fish and chips
love and bosoms
any more for the lighthouse
sorry, no vacancies
another one for the road
Dirk Bogarde

wipe your feet
no baths before ten
the rates
the rent
the rates
the rent
death
life

LIGHTS OUT

Production Notes

PRODUCTION NOTES

The Children's Crusade

The Children's Crusade in 1212 is fact. Stephen was twelve years old; he believed he could save Jerusalem from the Saracens who would bow down before God's innocent children. He had visions that told him the Mediterranean Sea would part to allow the Crusade through dry-shod. Many people wanted to believe him and so had faith in the Crusade. Thirty thousand children assembled at Vendôme. By the time they reached Marseilles, there were far fewer. Some had lost heart, some had lost their way, some had lost their lives: it was a hot, droughty summer. Yet there were enough left to fill the seven ships cruelly offered to take them to the Holy Land, though the children were unaware of their actual destination.

The play is based on the first-part of Henry Treece's novel, *The Children's Crusade*, which is strongly recommended for further reading. The story is interwoven with the personal agony of the Hermit (old Gerard) who, as the narrator, stands outside the action. He controls the events like the 'Ancient Mariner', holding the audience's attention compulsively. This part requires strong characterization to convey the profound suffering and aged dignity of the man. Robert de Beauregard is a blunt, bullying squire, representing the intolerance of arrogant adults to the young. He understands his son no more than Stephen, and his alliance with the spokesman of the Church, Brother Martin, is a condescension to an inferior. He dominates the opening scene and is responsible for imparting much of the background information about Stephen's Crusade. Stephen is a fascinating character to act. How to balance so many contradictory traits in a youth obsessed by a vision, to convey his megalomania and his vulnerability without making him unlikeable – these are problems that the young actor must grapple with. Seated in his hand-cart, Stephen can be seen to dominate, but his voice must also ring out with the rough edge of the peasant. It is a good idea to give him a northern accent, to accentuate his origins and his contrast to nobler-born characters. Yet this leader of youth must also be capable of childish spleen and instant collapse of morale. The young Gerard clearly hero-worships Stephen, but he is no weakling; he enthusiastically seeks both adventure and service of a worthy cause. Stephen's condemnation of killing after the camp-fire fight makes a strong impression on him and explains his horror of the murder at the end. The Piper provides a sinister echo of Hamelin's magic tempter, though he is fictitious; the two Merchants, however, were real enough, and Henry Treece writes that a few years after this Crusade both were hanged publicly for attempting to kidnap the Emperor Frederick for the Saracens. The villainy of these characters is obvious but their protestations of faith and kindness must seem genuine enough to justify the children's faith in them. The Piper should not be characterized as Browning's Pied Piper; he is much more cunning and calculating. Yet he has a certain charm; to the children he is both protector and guide and he must be adept on his pipe to lead the children on their way and to entertain them. He is grotesque (perhaps stressed by some physical deformity) but seems reformed into goodness. In performance, the Piper has responsibility for many of the cues and he controls much of the action.

As first performed the cast was nearly one hundred, and indeed the number of Crusaders is virtually limitless! The grown-up parts (mainly villainous) were played by adults, and this had the advantage of emphasizing the extraordinary conflict between young and old that lies at the heart of this play. A further topical allusion, referring to the 'beautiful' Crusade, has been written into the historical scene for dramatic effect, but the rebellion of the young against the establishment is ageless, and children carrying flowers, singing of their beautiful crusade (and wearing long hair) do not seem inappropriate to medieval times.

The movement of the Crusaders as they march may present problems if space is restricted. The idea is to produce a never-ending flow of marchers, perhaps entering from two of the four corner-ways and leaving by one exit route. Thus the children proceed across the arena and round behind one side of the audience to make a continual chain. If the staging does not allow this circular movement, the children should march round the arena or stage without fully leaving it. Stephen's hand-cart is important dramatically, if only because it allows him to stand above his followers; its usefulness ends after the camp-fire fight scene during which it could be taken off.

The two songs for the Crusaders are contrasted in mood; the first song is a rousing march, the second more lyrically plaintive. As the march is sung more than once, whistling or humming can provide some variation, when the Crusaders begin to tire on their journey. Both tunes are medieval (see note on p. 107 for details), the words being written to fit the melodies. To aid the marchers a small percussion group is useful, either situated near the first entrance route (kettle drum, side drum, glockenspeil and cymbal) or marching with them.

The middle section of the play is deliberately left for improvisation; its duration depends on how the producer cares to treat it. This camp-fire scene shows the children without adults present (the Piper sits apart in the shadows, providing

H

music unobtrusively). Freedom of expression is to be encouraged, but the improvisations must integrate with the text. So any tendency to use modern slang should be discouraged and the story-line must relate to the basic situation. Thus, it starts with pitching camp and although much can then happen, it must end with Stephen breaking up a fight.

A recommended procedure to build up the improvisations is:

First phase: about twenty-five principal Crusaders are to occupy the main arena (many others will be bedding down in the gangways and offstage). These principals are separated into four groups which gradually emerge as the Crusaders disperse, fetch wood, start a fire and settle down. One Crusader sings a nostalgic folk-song as the scene is set.

Second phase: the children begin to talk; the subject-matter can be resolved through discussion, but four main themes seem appropriate:

1. discussion of the ardours of the journey
2. argument about ways to deal with the Saracens
3. comment on the leader, Stephen
4. reminiscence about home compared with camp-life.

Each group should develop one of these themes, establishing its own pattern of words and business. The producer then interweaves the four group patterns so that talk and movement flow interestingly between the four parts of the arena. Food and drink are distributed meanwhile.

Third phase: a simple dance begins, perhaps between two, accompanied by the Piper and other Crusaders clapping to the rhythm. In the middle of this, the pretext for the squabble starts – possibly one boy, sent to fetch water, returns to find his own cup drained and begins to accuse another boy. One action leads to another and the dance stops on the outbreak of violence.

Fourth phase: the fight starts with threats and grimaces; then one boy is pushed over and gradually more are drawn in. It ends with one Crusader, Jean de Parchat, whose character should be shown during the talking, attempting to stab Gerard, only to be prevented by Stephen who takes the blow. To keep the fight 'tidy', the movement may be formalized into a number of poses which each couple or trio of fighters has to work on. There could be, for example, a sequence of ten moves to the beat of a drum or cymbal.

Lighting by spotlight is desirable for the opening and closing scenes with the Hermit. Some suitably unobtrusive music to create the time-distancing effect and sombre mood is recommended here, for example, the opening bars of Sibelius' fourth Symphony. When the marching of the Crusaders is 'frozen', perhaps to the sound of a cymbal roll, a lighting change will help create the effect of timelessness. Only the red glow of the fire is necessary when amongst the sleeping Crusaders the Hermit moves carrying a lantern. As usual in arena production, the acting area can be bare of properties or settings. But there is plenty of scope for colourful and authentic costumes, banners and other properties carried by the characters.

(*Note*: First song: 'Barrow-Boy's Song.' Carmina edition, No. 7, published by A. A. Kalmus, Ltd., 2–3 Fareham St., London, W.1.

Second song: 'Winder, wie ist nu dein kraft' – N. von Reuenthal. Song No. 10 in *Songs of the Ages* published by Schofield and Sims, Huddersfield.)

Colombo

This is a stirring drama of the high seas, benefitting from the
freedom of movement that the arena provides. The voyage of
Columbus to discover the western route to the Indies is one of
the great triumphs of historical exploration, albeit a lucky one.
Everyone knows the basic story, yet Columbus himself
remains a somewhat obscure hero, possibly because he did not
intend to discover a new world; but his deliberate challenge of
the unknown seas in the fifteenth century was as daring and
courageous as a modern astronaut's exploration of space, and
really far more hazardous in view of the incompetent prepara-
tions and his untrustworthy companions. He had one domin-
ant conviction and the play focuses dramatic interest on this
obsessive faith that drove him on and enabled him to defeat
the pessimism and hostility of other men.

As portrayed in this play, Columbus is a solitary figure,
entering on occasion to quell the restlessness of his crew or to
argue with his captain, but always aloof and introspective. He
is no ideal hero, and there should be a rough edge and im-
patient nervousness in his manner to others. The men are in
awe of him but they distrust his judgement. At the climax, it
must seem that Columbus might fail to win the support of the
frightened crew. There is a dramatic pause before the
drummer-boy steps forward to swing the balance back in
Columbus' favour. As the Old Sailor says in his opening
speech, if it hadn't been for him when he was young, history
might have been very different.

The supporting characters are firmly drawn and demand

strong dramatic performances to capture the harsh and sometimes brutal human relationships. The captain is a likeable
plain, honest sailor; his momentary defection at the climax of
the play must be seen to be a difficult decision for him to make.
The Pinzon brothers are more sophisticated and courtly in
their manner, but their shrewd practical sense predominates.
Their argument about Columbus' voyage clearly sketches the
background detail and the facts should be stressed convincingly.

The storm is the most exciting part of the drama and this
gives the crew plenty of chances for intelligent acting. The
crew has already created the atmosphere of a ship at sea.
Heaving on ropes to the rhythm of a shanty at the start,
crowding round Juan to enjoy the spilling of blood, they have
conveyed the routine and boredom of their lives. Now they
take over the arena with robust confidence. The producer
must plan the action carefully. Obviously a good sound-track
of a storm at sea is needed, full of thunder, crashing waves and
howling winds. The interpretation of the storm chant is
variable. It can be treated as choral speech, the crew either
standing in stylized grouping to speak it or pausing between
actions to utter snatches of the chant before resuming their
work, while the drummer-boy exhorts them. Indeed, it could
be sung similarly. Alternatively, the singing or choral speaking
can be recorded and played over the storm while the crew
goes about its work; this is probably the simpler method, for
it allows the crew to concentrate on activity. The chant lends
itself to improvisation as a free-flowing ballad, using the
drummer-boy's beat and his voice counterpointing the deeper
voices and the storm effects.

Amidst the organized chaos of the tumult, hanging and
swinging ropes (particularly if they can bear the weight of a
man) are useful. There should be a pattern of sailors running

in several directions, lights flashing, ropes pulled, dragged and swung around the arena, voices crying and shouting and sudden clusters of men hauling ropes vertically or horizontally. If there is a central ship's wheel, the man at the wheel must stagger dramatically, controlling the sideways movement of the crew flung to the deck by the ship's rolling. Columbus, sick and pale, can be hustled off, while the captain and the bos'n shout their orders. Eventually, at the climax of the storm the crew is sent sprawling, the wheel unattended; as the storm subsides, the first Sailor becomes the spokesman of their fears. He must express the desperate hysteria of their terror full-bloodedly. When the final vindication of Columbus occurs, the crew must show the same team-work as they express relief and joy that land has been sighted.

The arena can effectively be set with low rostrums for this play. It is recommended that there are three basic units. The central rostrum could hold a ship's wheel (or similar nautical symbol); the action revolves round this and this is the *Santa Maria*'s centre. Two side platforms flank this; they serve as speaking points for the Pinzon brothers who sail in the *Pinta* and the *Nina*. Ropes angled across the acting area and rigging casting shadows from spotlights are also effective. As so often in arena production, the rapid sweep of action, four exits and entrances, the adroit switching of attention at close range and the imaginative appeal of open spaces unlocalized by scenery, contribute to the dramatic impact of the play.

The Chimney Sweeps

Anthony Delves wrote this play at the age of seventeen. His sixth-form reading of William Blake's poems and of historical records of child-labour in early industrial Britain led him to dramatize the basic issues in a play requiring strong performances and delicate changes of mood. The story is about a runaway apprentice-sweep, but the most important character is really the narrator. A visionary man, William Blake, born into this 'great Wem' of expansion and deprivation, could see the pity and terror of it all; frustrated and impotent in his desire to change society, he was driven into his private world of poetry and painting. The play shares Blake's bitter despair and loving care of people, and his writings are used to dramatic effect in the narrative. He is much more than a narrator; his character develops through the action of the play.

Jacob Sharp is a flamboyant antagonist to Blake, but he is no melodramatic villain. His innate cunning is disguised by a façade of bluster or humility, depending on his adversary, but he has a full-blooded zest for his life that gains him some sympathy, and his family life, with the robust Rosie and spoilt son, Ruff, is a happy one. The Priest, to whom Sharp can turn for support, expresses the official Church attitude to the poor and needy; as such, though not likeable, he must be played earnestly and not caricatured. The Paupers are wily and shifty but they clearly state one view of the social situation, that it is better to slave than starve; they are pathetic victims of circumstance. Similarly the Parents must be seen as weak but well-meaning for their son. It is necessary to appreciate that

Blake, when he protests about the selling of children into virtual slavery, is confronting not simply evil people but the whole social framework. Hence the intensity of his symbolic ravings about the crushing of Albion (England) when the children dance in the streets, and in the final poem. He is aware that he is powerless to change things.

The characterization of the young apprentices should be based partly on the idiosyncrasies of the actors. Shiner is more mature in manner; he takes a pride in leading the apprentices and seems a hard nut, but there is a yearning for security and love behind the bitterness. The boys present a fierce exterior but at heart they are lonely. Above all they are loyal to each other and accept Ned as one of the group despite their initial hostility. Ned needs a plaintive face; his is a passive role, but he has to convey much through his gestures and facial expressions. Tom and Will are less aggressive than the others; they must be able to express the lyrical joy of the poem they speak. In performance, the speaking of Blake's poems does not seem incongruous to the children who, up to this point, have spoken with colloquial directness. If care is taken to create a strong aggressive mood as they crowd round Ned, the ensuing calm as they relent and leave him sobbing provides an appropriate atmosphere for the opening lines of Blake's poem. The second 'Chimney Sweep' poem, coming at the height of the boys' pathetic vision of a better world, harmonizes with the rapture that the speakers feel.

The scenes change rapidly and there should be no delay as characters enter while others depart. Dramatic contrasts are effective: thus, Blake goes out protecting the Paupers in contrast to Sharp who enters brutally treating the young boy, Ned. The arena should be kept bare; properties can be taken on and off by the performers. The hand-cart is an important property. It allows a clear distinction between Master and

Apprentices, it gives dramatic force to the sweeps' journey through London, and as a hearse it adds much pathos to the ending, with Ned lying on the sooty cloths and tools of his trade. The cart should be embellished with the name – Jacob Sharp, Master Sweep. The dance in the street need not be too formally executed (the boys are hardly prepared for it) and some simple Morris dance format, centred on the lord and lady sweeps, is indicated. Ruff plays a lively, rhythmic tune; the clapping or drumming of others (such as the Paupers) will help capture the mood.

The most difficult moment for the apprentices is probably the arrival at Longford House. By their reactions and facial expressions the boys must convey the size and grandeur of the building that confronts them. The Footman must by his condescension and his anxiety about the chimney-sweeping imply the presence of an aristocratic above-stairs world. He should not be played simply as a comic fop. During the events surrounding Ned's death offstage, an impression of confusion must be achieved through rapid exits and entrances, shouts and exclamations off and on stage; there must be tension between the avaricious Sharp, the scheming Bessie, the officious Footman and the hysterical boys in order to keep the audience's attention riveted on the arena. The entrance of Ned's body must seem a dreadful climax to the turmoil that the audience has witnessed. The final funeral procession is a stern tragic spectacle and should not be rushed.

The Tale of the Four Winds

This fantasy is particularly suitable for playing to young audiences, for children can take part by acting some of the characters and the audience participates in the 'blowing' of the four winds. Although the story is a romantic fairy-tale, the ending is not necessarily the traditional happy-ever-after. That depends on the audience's reactions!

The Chinese style of drama has a subtle charm compounded of sophisticated ritual and naïve improvisation. The audience accepts the formality and simplicity, but it expects elegance and style in the playing. There are three different styles at work. The four Winds, exotic and hieratic, need to create an oriental aura; they do this not so much by assuming sing-song intonations in their speech as by moving and gesticulating to a solemn ritual. The two male Winds could use violent, angular gestures, the female Winds more gentle and pliant, but all must harmonize in certain set poses. The arrival of the Emperor and his entourage introduces a different style. The characterization is exaggerated and somewhat grotesque, the Court's inhumanity perhaps emphasized by half-face masks. There is elaborate protocol and pomp in this scene, with much bowing and kneeling, but it is not quite the comic Mikado world and although there is plenty of fun in the mincing, fawning capering around the Emperor, there should be more vulgarity than delicacy in the movements. The Emperor himself is too boisterous to be an inscrutable mandarin; he is a rather charming monster and his large wife has him well tamed. The broad satire about political intriguers needs to be played for laughs, but of course in contrast the underlying fear of the 'lost prince' must produce moments of sudden stillness. The only time that the Emperor moves to formal ritualized steps is during his fight with the Kitchen-boy.

The boy stands in contrast to the courtiers; poorly dressed (certainly with no mask if these are worn by courtiers), he finds a happier environment amongst the mountain people (who also wear no masks). He never speaks but he has to move well, particularly during the miming of his escape from the Emperor. With the mountain people, the third style becomes established. Natural grace and beauty are evident in their dance-movement; the oriental (Balanese) manner is indicated but the dancing should be free-flowing. The Princess should be gracious and charming, but very much of royal blood.

Emphasis has been placed on dance, mime and general movement because the play is very much a musical. The little Chinese orchestra provides the accompaniment. The music score, composed by John York is in the 'Chinese' style; it is not difficult and is specially written for young recordists and tympanists. Basically there is need for first, second and third recordists, a chief percussionist and his assistant. Apart from sound effects during the action of the play, there are set dances for: the Vultures; the Mountain People; the Song for the Princess; and the final Dance of Triumph. Copies of the score may be obtained direct from John York, B.Mus., G.G.S.M. c/o the Grammar School, Eastbourne, Sussex.

The arena should be kept free of properties: the Emperor sits on a low seat or cushion taken on and off; the Winds use a blue strip of cloth for a river (which can be laid along one side of the arena after the Boy has crossed it) and a silken cord or rope; three hobby-horses, with gay eastern figure-heads, are used for the chase; the Jester discovers the curious golden ball containing a lotus flower. Otherwise, the attention is on costumes, masks and head-pieces (the four Winds should have elaborate and appropriate head-gear). There are golden opportunities for beautiful designs!

Each side of the arena 'in the round' represents the North, South, East and West; members of the audience in the front rows of each side must be provided with wind sound-effect-instruments which are used on the instructions of the four Winds. The latter carry emblematic sticks with which to control their attendant spirit sounds. When all four winds are 'blowing', it can sound like anything from a gale to a hurricane! Four such sound instruments are:

1. empty bottles for blowing across (North Wind)
2. sand-paper blocks (South Wind)
3. small triangles with strikers (East Wind)
4. Morris dance bells on cords (West Wind)

The play has been designed to allow 'instant' performance before young audiences. There are certain roles which require little or no rehearsal; these are to be acted by volunteers from the audience. The Kitchen-boy never speaks but he must act and mime well. He moves under the instructions of characters who are with him, but he should be told beforehand what he must do. The Princess has one short speech which could be read if necessary; the Ladies-in-Waiting control her moves on stage. The Retinue of Maidens (the Mountain People) can process on and off with the Ladies-in-Waiting, following a basic dance step in their movements. Costumes, mainly kimonos, must be provided.

From experience of touring primary schools with the play, it is advisable to ask for the parts of Princess, Kitchen-boy and Retinue of Maidens to be arranged beforehand. If these children are then briefed thirty minutes before the performance this is sufficient. The two Ladies-in-Waiting (who should be good dancers for they play also the parts of the Vultures) can instruct the girls; and the East and West Winds can show the boy his movements. Meanwhile, the audience in the front rows may like to try out their wind sound-effects in unison under the guidance of the North and South Winds.

Under Beachy Head

This play is a light-hearted portrait of a seaside resort, recognizably Eastbourne as written, but appropriate to any coastal holiday town at the height of the season. It was scripted with the help of middle-school pupils, some improvising the action, others contributing ideas or dialogue. There is clearly a debt to *Under Milk Wood*, the play for Voices by Dylan Thomas – and the title recognizes this. The characterization, however, is typically English and smacks of seaside saltiness and boarding-house holidays.

The play has its own arena structure and the producer must first make his cast appreciate the experimental teamwork that underlies the action. The Narrator moves freely on and off, varying the direction of his speaking and holding the audience in his spell. The characters come to life or subside under his instructions. Skill in pointing the wit and creating the moods of each scene is essential. But the Narrator must never be obtrusive and once he has set the action moving he should move out and appear next, perhaps, at another place.

The scene changes are effected with a minimum of fuss; the actors simply make the necessary adjustments as part of their characters. There is first the dream sequence, with characters lying in a pattern of sleepers on the floor. They lie in one of two halves of the arena – the residents at one end (Mr and Mrs Thyme, Captain Cod, Revd Josiah Pontiff) and the visitors at Seaview at the other end (Mr and Mrs Tubb, and sons, Mr and Mrs Honey, Mr and Mrs Ponsonby, Mr Warbledon and Emily Brown). At the centre of the radiating sleepers lie Mr and Mrs Puffin, the proprietors of Seaview. Benny Gill, the Milkman, has the important task of linking these characters to the Narrator's description; he must time his moves between the sleepers skilfully, keeping as much as possible to the sides.

The first change is to the breakfast scene, and the residents quietly depart while the Seaview visitors rise and prepare their breakfast-tables and chairs in a circle. A dining trolley can be wheeled on by Mr Puffin to serve foodstuffs. At the end of this sequence, helped by Mrs Puffin's brisk manner and sound effects, the change to the beach is made by rapidly clearing the set. Visitors help by taking out chairs, tables and trays as the Narrator speaks. The shuffling dance that develops between four of the happy residents should create the holiday mood of the open beach scene. The visitors trail down to the beach, all facing the side of the arena that represents the sea. Arranged well, this makes a colourful and credible scene.

After the downpour, visitors and residents cross the arena in different directions, but establish eventually the Seaview and the residents' ends. Mrs Puffin stands at her end to greet the guests; one table and two chairs are sufficient for the restaurant scene. Finally, we return to the sleepers resuming their original positions, simply bringing on with them a blanket or sheet under which to lie.

Clearly, good lighting is of the utmost importance. Spotlights need to cover restricted acting areas, particularly in the night sequences. The actors' task is harder if these are not available, but the play's strength will lie mainly in the characterization. The technical aids of lighting and sound effects are less vital than the performers' skill in creating character. There are recognizable types here, but there are no caricatures; many of them are uncomplicated positive people who enjoy life, like Benny Gill and Captain Cod, but others are gently satirized, like the Thymes and the Revd. Josiah Pontiff. As for the visitors, they form a well-contrasted group, and there is plenty of scope for comedy and satire. They all have their private hopes and dreams; their struggles to make the right impression in social relationships provide comic contrasts. But there are hidden depths to some of them. Mr Warbledon is a pathetic person in his loneliness; and the gulf that separates Mr and Mrs Ponsonby must be acted between the lines they speak. Furthermore, the comic business of the Tubb family on the beach indicates that there are plenty of opportunities for mime and original ideas.